SpringerBriefs in Political Science

SpringerBriefs present concise summaries of cutting-edge research and practical applications across a wide spectrum of fields. Featuring compact volumes of 50 to 125 pages, the series covers a range of content from professional to academic. Typical topics might include:

- A timely report of state-of-the art analytical techniques
- A bridge between new research results, as published in journal articles, and a contextual literature review
- A snapshot of a hot or emerging topic
- An in-depth case study or clinical example
- A presentation of core concepts that students must understand in order to make independent contributions

SpringerBriefs in Political Science showcase emerging theory, empirical research, and practical application in political science, policy studies, political economy, public administration, political philosophy, international relations, and related fields, from a global author community.

SpringerBriefs are characterized by fast, global electronic dissemination, standard publishing contracts, standardized manuscript preparation and formatting guidelines, and expedited production schedules.

More information about this series at https://link.springer.com/bookseries/8871

Ignas Kalpokas • Julija Kalpokiene

Deepfakes

A Realistic Assessment of Potentials, Risks, and Policy Regulation

Springer

Ignas Kalpokas (iD)
Department of Public Communication
Vytautas Magnus University
Kaunas, Lithuania

Julija Kalpokiene
Faculty of Law
Vytautas Magnus University
Kaunas, Lithuania

ISSN 2191-5466 ISSN 2191-5474 (electronic)
SpringerBriefs in Political Science
ISBN 978-3-030-93801-7 ISBN 978-3-030-93802-4 (eBook)
https://doi.org/10.1007/978-3-030-93802-4

This Springer imprint is published by the registered company Springer Nature Switzerland AG
The registered company address is: Gewerbestrasse 11, 6330 Cham, Switzerland

Contents

Chapter 1
Introduction

The intention behind this book is to analyse the use and potential impact of deepfakes—primarily images and videos that can involve both creating artificial representations of non-existent individuals and showing actual individuals doing things they did not do. As such, deepfakes pose an obvious threat of manipulation and, unsurprisingly, have been the subject of a great deal of alarmism in both the news media and academic articles. Hence, this book sets out to critically evaluate potential threats by analysing human susceptibility to manipulation and then using that as a backdrop for a discussion of actual and likely uses of deepfakes. In contrast to the usual threat narrative, this book puts forward a multi-sided picture of deepfakes, including by exploring the potential to use deepfakes and underlying or adjacent technologies in creative domains ranging from film and advertisement to painting. The challenges posed by deepfakes are further evaluated with regards to present or forthcoming legislation and other regulatory measures. Finally, deepfakes are placed within a broader cultural and philosophical context, focusing primarily on posthumanist thought. Hence, this book is explicitly conceived as a concise but, nevertheless, well-rounded treatment of deepfakes.

In the most general sense, deepfakes should be contextualised as a type of synthetic media, i.e. media that, instead of capturing the 'real' world, is produced by AI-powered (or, at least, AI-adjacent) digital tools based on training data. Hence, it is not the 'real' world but data that is represented. A very similar definition is also provided by Schick (2020, p. 8), for whom '[a] deepfake is a type of "synthetic media", meaning media (including images, audio and video) that is either manipulated or *wholly generated* by AI' (Schick, 2020, p. 8); likewise, for Whittaker et al. (2020, p. 91), synthetic media are 'automatically and artificially generated or manipulated media' that include synthesized audio, virtual reality, and various forms of advanced image creation (see also Kalpokas, 2021). A very similar definition is also provided by the European Parliamentary Research Service (2021, p. I), framing deepfakes as 'manipulated or synthetic audio or visual media that seem authentic, and which feature people that appear to say or do something they have never said or done, produced using artificial intelligence techniques, including

I. Kalpokas, J. Kalpokiene, *Deepfakes*, SpringerBriefs in Political Science, https://doi.org/10.1007/978-3-030-93802-4_1

machine learning and deep learning'. Hence, the artificial and manipulative aspects of this type of media feature constantly across definitions.

While the ability to manipulate (or wholly generate) audio-visual content is not new, what differentiates deepfakes and other present-day synthetic media from legacy techniques is their automated nature. While traditionally manipulation has been a laborious and time-consuming process that necessitated considerable skill, the automated production of synthetic media effectively 'outsources' the skill and labour to technology. Hence, as Gosse and Burkell (2020, p. 499) note, the availability of such tools 'democratizes a capacity that was historically related to experts in the entertainment industry: namely, the ability to create convincing fabricated video of people doing and saying things that did not happen in real life' (Gosse & Burkell, 2020, p. 499). In an almost identical fashion, for Bode et al. (2021, p. 2) '[t]he development of deepfakes represents a democratisation of access to sophisticated techniques of digital image manipulation, techniques previously the exclusive domain of high-end visual effects postproduction houses working for Hollywood studios'. Hence, there is a potentially broad use potential of the technology, both benevolent and malevolent.

Of course, neither deepfakes nor their increasing uptake in today's digital environment can be seen in isolation, disconnected from the broader underlying structures of supply and demand. The formation of 'a welcoming environment for deepfakes' involves, among other developments, 'the changing media landscapes by means of online sharing platforms; the growing importance of visual communication; and the growing spread of disinformation' (European Parliamentary Research Service, 2021, p. III). Additional matters that boost the uptake of deepfakes include a supply-and-demand infrastructure, such as marketplaces for requesting and acquiring deepfake content; increasing availability and commodification of deepfake tools, whereby little prior knowledge and ability is necessary for the use of deepfake generation software; the presence of deepfake-as-a-service companies that specialise in creation of (legitimate) deepfake content; and ever-decreasing requirement for input data, with only a handful of training examples sufficing to produce content of acceptable quality (European Parliamentary Research Service, 2021, p. 15). All that being taken into consideration, the increasing normalisation of deepfakes seems to be a natural and unavoidable development.

Even a cursory glance across the currently available literature on deepfakes reveals a rather stark picture—one of deepfakes as something specifically and (almost) exclusively used for disinformation and misinformation or other nefarious uses (see, characteristically, Schick, 2020, p. 9). In fact, one can be led to believe that deepfakes may put us on a straight path towards 'Infocalypse'—a condition of the entire society being overwhelmed with misinformation and disinformation; according to such alarmist discourse, '[w]e are now facing a monumental and unprecedented crisis of mis- and disinformation' (Schick, 2020, p. 9). Similarly, although in less dramatic terms, the European Parliamentary Research Service's (2021, p. III) projection is that '[p]erhaps the most worrying societal trend that is fed by the rise of disinformation and deepfakes is the perceived erosion of trust in news and information, confusion of facts and opinions, and even "truth" itself'. While at least some of the fears inherent in such assertions are well-grounded, as argued in this book, deepfakes are a significantly more complex phenomenon that stands at the intersection of a rapidly evolving relationship between humans and technology. In this sense, one could at least partly agree with Schick's (2020, p. 26) assertion that '[w]e are at the early stages of an AI revolution that will completely transform representations of reality through media'; however, as demonstrated in the eighth chapter of this book, this 'revolution' must, instead, be seen within the context of broader philosophical concerns that, among other things, problematise the very notion of reality to be represented.

Likewise, deepfakes put into question some long-held truisms about the human self. Not least, they disentangle the human self and the human face as never before. While this relationship has been already put into question before by earlier tools and techniques for visual representation, from painting to photography, the artificial generation of faces in case of deepfakes takes the matter a whole lot further by decentring the human face as an object of representation and replacing it with data-based generation. In this way, as Bode et al. (2021, p. 1) observe, '[t]hough long fundamental to portraiture, cinema, television, and surveillance, the human face is emerging as the central object of critical ambivalence in the digital era'. Moreover, the trend toward destabilisation of the face and its growing shift towards an independent life unconstrained by the human self (and, in case of malevolent deepfakes, even undermining the human self) is more than clear. Under such circumstances, 'the face as image and its intimate, inviolable connection to the human subject is becoming more and more fluid and unstable' (Bode et al., 2021, p. 1). Hence, more than just a new digital tool or an additional security threat, synthetic media and their underlying technologies must be seen as representative of a deeper shift concerning the human self and its place in the world.

Overall, it is likely that the lived experience of the world will shift away from a clearly defined and objectively graspable ideal of Western modernity towards a more anarchic and intangible one (a development that, following the posthumanist perspective outlined in the eighth chapter of this book, is not necessarily something to be lamented). However, this is likely to be a gradual process and not the result of a one-off watershed moment that should shake taken-for-granted assumptions about the world—a kind of 'deepfake 9/11'. Likewise, such a transformation will not be the result of deepfakes alone but will result from the broader changes to the notion of 'reality' altogether, including its growing personalisation and 'de-tangibilisation', or virtualisation (development of new immersive virtual worlds, or the 'metaverse' is likely to play an important role as well). Overall, then, deepfakes are characteristic representations of fundamental changes and shifts—but they need to be assessed realistically as well.

Structure of the Book

The book opens with a discussion of fake news as a characteristic feature of today's information environment. As most of the existing literature on deepfakes focuses on their use for disinformation, including as an amplifying factor for fake news, it is important to get to the root of the phenomenon. Hence, the chapter will explore the structural conditions leading to the rise of fake news, primarily focusing on the transformations in today's media environment and the changing information sphere. Also, the basic features of fake news, their distribution, and uptake are analysed and some of the dominant trends are identified. The overall picture that emerges is one in which technological affordances and human propensities merge to collectively produce a new societal development—a pattern that will, it transpires, repeat itself, with minor variations, throughout this book.

The third chapter of the proposed book analyses the factors that contribute to human susceptibility to disinformation and manipulation. The matters assessed range from psychological biases and group dynamics to algorithmic governance of information, common across the domains of news and social media, and the mediatization of everyday life. The purpose here is to critically assess the vulnerabilities existing in the fabric of societies that deepfakes could be targeted at and to evaluate the type and quality of deepfakes necessary to cause social and political harm. This will draw, to a large extent, on the extant literature on disinformation, post-truth, and conspiracy theories, but particular care will be taken to elucidate their connections with deepfakes.

In the subsequent chapter, attention shifts towards establishing the characteristics of deepfakes. It is not meant to be a technical description and will cover the underlying technology, such as Generative Adversarial Networks (GANs), in a way that does not necessitate any background in IT or AI. Factors enabling and limiting the creation of deepfakes are assessed and weighed against each other. The chapter concludes with a typology of deepfake uses, including both benevolent and malevolent ones. The ultimate aim is to lay out the key premises and core functionality while also contextualising the underlying technology within the broader deep learning/Artificial Intelligence (AI) framework.

In the fifth chapter of this book, the aim is to discuss and critically assess the prevalent discourse on deepfakes, which usually contains highly alarmist overtones. One frequently encounters references to destabilisation and undermining of truth, fake news on steroids or an upcoming infodemic (or infocalypse) when engaging with the extant discussions of deepfakes in both academic and professional literature as well as in the news media. Such representations of threats are subsequently contrasted and compared against the characteristics of deepfakes and societal vulnerabilities covered in the previous chapters. A more realistic threat landscape that thereby emerges is composed not of high-profile manipulative attacks but primarily pertains to a more generalised epistemic anarchy (an advanced stage of pan-society distrust) as well as harassment of activists, investigative journalists, and the like. In other words, there still are threats, but in other places than most extant literature would suggest.

The sixth chapter covers a less-often represented aspect of deepfakes and adjacent technologies, such as Creative Adversarial Networks (a variation of GANs, aimed as combining recognisability and originality of computer-generated output)—namely, algorithmic generation of art. While this is only a subset of computer creativity, it is, nevertheless, one that has already produced monetizable results, including a GAN-created artwork having been sold at an auction. All this necessitates a discussion of algorithmic creativity more broadly and of the ways in which this new way of originating artwork potentially challenges some of the core assumptions about humanity. No less importantly, this discussion also raises important questions about agency and the human-machine relationship that will be of particular importance in the eighth chapter of this book.

Having outlined the diverse uses of deepfakes and underlying technologies in the previous chapters, in Chap. 7 the authors move towards analysing existing and proposed regulation of deepfakes in key jurisdictions, such as EU, US, and UK (to the extent that such regulation and/or initiatives exist). Primary matters of concern include manipulative use of deepfakes, non-consensual synthetic pornography, and data use. Questions are raised as to the most effective form of regulation and the regulator itself: whether state legislation or the policies of online platforms (self-regulation) should be favoured. Finally, the matter of enforcement is brought to the fore in terms of jurisdictional issues and technicalities, such as the balance between human judgement and that of autonomous AI-enabled detection tools.

Lastly, the final substantive chapter of this book contextualises deepfakes within the broader strand of posthumanist thinking, particularly in terms of de-privileging human reason, cognition, and creativity and countering anthropocentric visions of the world. This also involves positioning deepfakes within the broader anxieties as to the role and future of humans vis-à-vis AI but doing so in a constructive manner. In this way, deepfakes, and the prevalent discourse on them, transpires to be not an isolated phenomenon, but part of a broader transformation of the human encounter with their environment. In this way, it becomes evident that the alarmist discourse clearly misses the deep embeddedness of not just deepfakes but also broader digital data-based technologies within human existence—a fallacy that needs to be rectified by providing a rich philosophical background deepfakes as a matter for contemporary society.

References

Bode, L., Lees, D., & Golding, D. (2021). Editorial: The digital face and deepfakes on screen. *Convergence: The International Journal of Research into New Media Technologies*. https://doi.org/10.1177/13548565211034044

European Parliamentary Research Service. (2021). *Tackling deepfakes in European Policy*, https://www.europarl.europa.eu/thinktank/en/document.html?reference=EPRS_STU(2021)690039

Gosse, C., & Burkell, J. (2020). Politics and porn: How news media characterizes problems presented by deepfakes. *Critical Studies in Media Communication, 37*(5), 497–511.

Kalpokas, I. (2021). Problematising reality: The promises and perils of synthetic media. *SN Social Sciences, 1*(1), 1–11.

Schick, N. (2020). *Deep fakes and the infocalypse: What you urgently need to know*. Monoray.

Whittaker, L., Kietzmann, T. C., Kietzmann, J., & Dabirian, A. (2020). 'All around me are synthetic faces': The mad world of ai-generated media. *IT Professional, 22*(5), 90–99.

Chapter 2
Fake News: Exploring the Backdrop

In order to better understand the immediate context of deepfakes and, in particular, of its most widely discussed application—disinformation—one must start with fake news. However, there immediately is a problem because any discussion of fake news has become very difficult, almost to the point of being counter-productive, precisely due to the ubiquity of the term. Indeed, one could broadly agree with Jankowicz's (2020, p. xx) observation that the term 'fake news' has been used so much that 'it has all but lost meaning'. Nevertheless, it must still be admitted that the current information environment appears to offer a favourable climate for deliberately manufactured false information to spread, and this is a key characteristic that determines both the use and perception of deepfakes.

One of the main structural factors enabling fake news is the automation and algorithmisation of the information environment. For example, Seubert and Becker (2019, p. 933) stress that '[s]ocial media newsfeeds are personalized by algorithms; computer programmes decide on the relevance of news – even our "friends" will not reach us if the technical automats choose their posts to be irrelevant'. Similarly, Citton (2019, p. 29) opts for a play of words by substituting the social media ecosystem with an echosystem courtesy to the former operating 'as an echo chamber whose reverberations "occupy" our minds (in the military sense of the term)' to the effect that 'most of the time, we think [. . .] only what is made to resonate in us in the media vault by the echoes with which it surrounds us'. The ensuing echosystem is, therefore, defined as *'an infrastructure of resonances conditioning our attention to what circulates around, through and within us'*, drawing users' attention towards where others, judged to be similar, had previously drawn theirs (Citton, 2019, pp. 29, 84). For Sunstein (2018, p. 3), meanwhile, algorithms are tools that are bound to know users better than they do themselves, leveraging any uncovered proclivities to push content that is, consequently, bound to be believed in.

If one follows the above line of argument, it comes as no surprise that, for example, Nadler et al. (2018) call the system of algorithmic content governance a 'Digital Influence Machine'. The latter is said to incorporate 'a set of overlapping technologies for surveillance, targeting, testing, and automated decision-making'

I. Kalpokas, J. Kalpokiene, *Deepfakes*, SpringerBriefs in Political Science,
https://doi.org/10.1007/978-3-030-93802-4_2

with the aim to maximise the convince-ability of the message by making it possible to 'reach the right person with the right message at the right time' (Nadler et al., 2018, pp. 4–5). And even though most of the major social media platforms have by now banned explicitly political targeting, it has been demonstrated that finding non-political attribute proxies for explicitly political orientation is not particularly difficult (see e.g. Cotter et al., 2021). Hereby, the user becomes encapsulated in their (and their peers') previous behaviour and information/ideological choices, leaving no room for 'openness and curiosity' (Maddalena & Gili, 2020, pp. 80–81). Indeed, from this standpoint, it makes sense to assert that the disinformation and fake news-filled echo chambers thereby created 'make democracies ungovernable' (Benkler et al., 2018, p. 5). While such alarm calls may, in fact be pushing the matter too far—the actual evidence of algorithmically induced information silos, or 'filter bubbles' is mixed (for more critical perspectives, see e.g., Bruns, 2019; Brotherton, 2020)—it is, nevertheless, the case that even if only a fraction of the population is affected—those who are the most susceptible to a particular message—the balance of power might still be tipped (see e.g. Kalpokas & Kalpokiene, 2021). Moreover, while it is clear that 'algorithms expose people to political news that is most popular among the people that make up the online environment that they are frequenting', the actual effects—such as the intensity with which counter-attitudinal information is filtered out—'will depend on the partisan composition of the reference group that drives the ranking' (Shmargad & Klar, 2020, p. 424). In other words, the more moderate the reference group, the more moderate will be the effects and, likewise, the more radical the group, the stronger the filtering will be.

It must also be stressed that the above siloisation exceeds information consumption; in fact, as Ammerman (2019, p. 37) demonstrates, convergence of data analytics, programmatic ad buying, novel content targeting techniques, and growing platformisation means that the intended message can be delivered to the target in diverse ways simultaneously, making sure that it is almost unavoidably noticed and that the target is immersed within what is (algorithmically) understood as fitting existing data patterns. In this way, one could reasonably assert that '[p]latforms do not reflect the social: they *produce* the social structures we live in' (van Dijck et al., 2018, p. 2) by way of establishing patterns and connections while also enabling and disabling behaviours. Crucially, with the ever-accelerating growth in the number of 'smart' connected devices, the data points that can be collected on every individual will become only more numerous and more revealing (Mazarr et al., 2019, p. 2). With individuals increasingly adopting a 'news-finds-me' perception, i.e. the (mistaken) belief that one can be sufficiently informed just by following a generic media diet without intentionally following and/or seeking the news (see e.g. Gil de Zúñiga et al., 2017, p. 118), personalisation of content supply becomes ever more dangerous from a societal perspective. And since it seems to be the case that the more people use social media and the more they encounter news serendipitously, the more they manifest the 'news-finds-me' perception (Strauß et al., 2021), audiences seem to be entering a vicious circle of increasing dependence on whatever circulates in their social networks, including fake news.

Moreover, it must be kept in mind that media use today is non-news-centric: news are 'all but completely interwoven with other types of information', as illustrated by the diversity of a typical smartphone 'checking cycle', which tends to involve 'news sites or apps, social media, dating apps, and so on all in one go'; likewise, in social media feeds, 'news is but one among many different information types' (Kormelink & Meijer, 2019, pp. 639–640). Even more ominously, in the oversaturated media environment, the very abundance of competing 'facts' has the effect of eroding trust in facts altogether (Lewandowsky et al., 2017, p. 355) as everything and anything could seemingly be true and supporting 'evidence' can always be found. This onslaught of diverse pieces of information, often mutually incompatible, is likely to at least induce some doubt, which is immediately conducive towards disinformation: as 'credible phenomena can seldom be proven absolutely', a 'rhetorical crack' is opened up for disinformation to start seeping in (O'Shaughnessy, 2020, p. 59). Notably, then, if the attitudes of individuals can be tampered with, even short of a complete wrapping within a sealed information environment, politics is at risk of turning into what Palano (2019) calls 'bubble democracy'. That is particularly the case in times of polarisation when clear-cut identities are being sought for and those seen as a threat are disconnected from (Bozdag, 2020, pp. 10–11). Hence, while filter bubbles are not an independent *cause* of polarisation, threat actors definitely can tap into them and thereby aggravate the situation.

Zuboff (2019) connects the provision of personalised content with what she calls 'surveillance capitalism'. As simultaneously an ideology and a business practice, surveillance capitalism not only transforms human experience into behavioural data but also, through the use of machine learning and other sophisticated technologies, manufactures 'prediction products' that can be sold on to actors lacking in data and analytic capacities but still intending to profit from prediction of future consumer behaviour (Zuboff, 2019, p. 8). The aim here is to be able to uncover the inner life of the target audiences in order to create personalised content that makes it impossible not to fall for the promoted message; in this way, knowledge of the present, prediction of the future, and personalisation of the offering really go hand-in-hand (Zuboff, 2019, pp. 254–255, 278), also leading to the audience *expectation* of me-centricity, as outlined in later in this book. In a similar manner, van Dijck et al. (2018, p. 41) focus on predictive analytics as 'the ability to predict future choices and trends on the basis of analyzing historical patterns of individual and aggregate data'. Unsurprisingly, Chandler (2019, p. 76) draws a specific connection between datafication and commodification by way of turning populations knowable in order to make them exploitable.

Similarly, with a more specific emphasis on communication, Hepp et al. (2018, pp. 5–6) stress that social dynamics 'no longer refer only to human communication, but also to the automatized accumulation of the data we produce while we use digital services for communication' to the effect that 'the social world becomes more and more constructed through datafication'. In this way, the algorithmic environment becomes an 'attention machine' that ultimately 'seeks to submit attention flows to needs and desires that will maximize financial returns' (Citton, 2019, p. 73). No less so, real-time big data analytics have become indispensable for political campaigns, providing insights for a more effective targeting of the electorate (van Dijck et al., 2018, p. 35) or the audience intended to be manipulated (Hendricks & Vestergaard, 2019, p. 13). Increasingly, with the development of AI capacities, mass personalisation of content—automatic generation of (different versions of) content to suit individual—or group-level data on psychological proclivities and potential information vulnerabilities—is becoming a feasible practice (Hermann, 2021). This is of particular relevance because, ultimately, if the audiences like something, they will ultimately come to believe in it, regardless of veracity (for an elaboration, see Kalpokas, 2018).

Another structural factor is the rise of the so-called 'attention economy' or 'like economy', which has effects on both information placement and attention paid. On the one hand, we can witness the rise of an entrepreneurial online self (see e.g. Courtenay-Smith, 2018) that ultimately thrives on attention in the form of likes, shares, and other forms of digital affirmation. It might well not be too far-fetched to assert, with Courtenay-Smith (2018, p. 119), that 'We live in a world where we have several gods: Google and the large social platforms. All of them reward content creation and publishing with visibility'. Therefore, in this age of a digital-first existence of the self, '[c]ontent distribution equals visibility and influence' (Courtenay-Smith, 2018, p. 119). Likewise, for Citton (2019, p. 70), in the algorithmic environment, 'you are valued at the value of the attention you are given'. Similarly, as emphasised by Vaidhyanathan (2018, pp. 50–51), '[w]e perform our tribal membership with what we post or share *on Facebook', generating social value through the content shared and by defending any such claims from detractors (thereby demonstrating group loyalty); ultimately, then, '[e]ven when we post and share demonstrably false stories and claims we do so to declare our affiliation, to assert that our social bonds mean more to us than the question of truth'. In the same manner, Ackland and Gwynn (2021, pp. 28–29) stress the importance of normative pressures, such as acceptance and group affirmation, in the spreading of fake news. This has an impact on user-generated or, at least, user-shared content that becomes oriented towards attention-maximisation, if necessary, at the expense of other attributes, such as veracity (Seubert & Becker, 2019, p. 933).

The same also applies to consumption—individuals tend to consume what is accepted and popular within the group to which they ascribe themselves (Kryston & Eden, 2021; see also Till, 2021, p. 1364). Moreover, it is crucial to keep in mind that audiences are not merely passive consumers of content, including fake news and other manipulatory messages, but are, instead, 'also active in its creation, modification, spread and amplification, often inadvertently furthering the agenda of propagandists whose messaging resonates with their worldview' (Wanless & Berk, 2020, p. 86) and, it must be also stressed, with the worldview of the referent peer groups whose attention is to be attracted and maintained. Notably, as repetition is one of the core attributes of perceived veracity (and if multiple individuals within a network share the same content, others are bound to encounter it repetitively), such sharing behaviour only further increases the uptake of fake news (Schwartz & Jalbert, 2021, p. 78). In other words, encounter with fake news is typically an act of prosumption, not mere consumption, rendering parts of the audience into

unwitting propagandists, engaging in reality construction in the adversary's preferred terms simply through their daily use of (especially) social media (Till, 2021,
pp. 1371–1372). Such 'participatory' disinformation allows a threat agent to extend
their capacities without directly engaging with every target audience, instead
reaching the intended recipients through their own online networks, thereby increasing reach exponentially through network effects (Wanless & Berk, 2020, p. 86; see
also Till, 2021, p. 1364).

On the other hand, attention becomes an increasingly scarce resource in today's
context of information overload. The latter is a consequence of a dramatic reduction
in the costs of spreading content, associated with digital and, particularly, social
media, which has caused a boom in communication. As sufficient attention cannot
be paid to the content encountered, individuals tend to opt for quick, often emotion-
centric solutions (as elaborated in the subsequent chapter). Indeed, as Doyle and
Roda (2019, p. 1) claim, 'our societies are living through a fundamental transformation in how we pay attention', particularly in the way in which scarcity of
attention 'is coupled with an overriding push by corporations and institutions to
capture, mobilize, and profit from attention'. The result is, therefore, that '[i]n the
twenty-first century, attention is perceived as bearing similarity to money: most of us
do not have enough of it, we seek more of it, but it is unequally distributed' (Doyle &
Roda, 2019, pp. 1–2). This drives the impetus, for legitimate and bogus content
providers alike, to double down on their efforts to prioritise attention capture over
everything else, including over the quality of their content.

Likewise, on the consumer side, the perception of time is fundamentally
transformed by way of compression and (perceived) urgency. As Chambers (2019,
p. 2) aptly puts it, 'technology compresses time to generate a sense of time expiring,
slipping away and "running out"', forcing users 'to multi-task mounting commit-
ments to the point of exhaustion'. In fact, not only individuals are experiencing
information overload due to the superabundance of information but also one can
witness the blurring of the distinction between reputable professional and amateur
narratives due to the lack of time and opportunity for double-checking. Similarly,
Harsin (2019: 100-101) writes about a 'fast, pleasure-packed but epistemically
vertiginous flow of perception' as the cause of 'confusion, false knowledge, and
an uptake of fake news' while Dahlgren (2018, p. 26) stresses 'high velocity and
dizzying excess'. Part of the matter is, of course, 'the shift from more-curated mass
media to less-curated Internet websites and uncurated social media', which 'permits
outright falsehoods to spread much faster and farther' (Libicki, 2017, p. 52) while
also releasing the floodgates for content of the most varied kind (and reliability),
thereby directly contributing to the overload. Indeed, the content that does best in
such circumstances is bite-sized and intuitively appealing (Syvertsen, 2020, p. 38),
even if it is fake.

Under the conditions of increasing volume and velocity of content, there is a
growing danger of falling for trolls (fully employed influence agents), bots, and other
disinformation actors that aim to simulate public opinion on a particular matter,
thereby dragging (at least the more susceptible parts of) the population along and
making them modify their behaviour in light of such a manufactured view of the

world (Pomerantsev, 2019, p. 81; see also Till, 2021, pp. 1364, 1368). Hence, we are facing a combination of increased ease with which content, including fake news, can be spread, the ensuing audience inability to pay sufficient attention, and the ensuing preference for easily accessible and consumable content; moreover, given that fake news manifest an inherent malleability (not being tied to a ground truth, they can be twisted in any way to suit target audience needs), the latter can be seen to have an inherent competitive advantage (Ackland & Gwynn, 2021; Schwartz & Jalbert, 2021; see also Kalpokas, 2018).

The rise of bots—defined, for example, by Woolley and Guilbeault (2017, p. 3) as 'automated software programs that operate on social media, written to mimic real people' represents one of the earlier waves of concern about online automated tools used to spread disinformation. Although Woolley and Guilbeault's emphasis on mimicking real people might be somewhat far-fetched (bots do not need to be fully realistic and convincing in order to disseminate a message or simulate public opinion—similarly, as will be argued later, to deepfakes), they do represent a broader concern about a lack of authenticity in online media that drives much or the contemporary disinformation/fake news discourse.

However, online disinformation and the deliberate spread of manipulatory fake news are at their most dangerous when coupled with the analytic and delivery capacity of data-rich and platform-savvy threat actors. It must be stressed, as Pomerantsev (2019, p. 209) does, that the multiplicity of the audience is the default starting point—people care about and are organised around interests that differ greatly; moreover, some individuals are more politically engaged than others—and, therefore, diverse strategies are necessary for reaching out to them. Hence, the availability of large data pools to identify the soft spots within a particular audience and the capacity to deliver content precisely to the particular segment of the population (e.g. by using social media's targeting services) are of the essence. However, similar practices are applicable not only to disinformation agents and other kinds of threat actors but also to conventional newsrooms where real-time audience data and popularity metrics are used to power content governance and placement algorithms (Zamith et al., 2020, p. 1769). Likewise, AI tools are often used to design and personalise the *content itself*, not just to direct it to the most appropriate audiences or to show existing audiences more of what they already like. In fact, as Ammerman (2019, p. 45) puts it, '[f]or a single advertising campaign, a machine can optimize millions of ad impressions with a hundred versions of message delivered in combination with a thousand different images targeting 50 different audiences in 10,000 locations to achieve the best results'. What really matters at this point is that every individual is increasingly targeted in ways 'dictated by a combination of marketing automation and machine learning – all designed to persuade us in increasingly sophisticated, imperceptible ways' while also learning what works and what does not from real-life data (Ammerman, 2019, pp. 46, 110).

Crucially, the aim of threat actors is typically not full persuasion—that would raise the bar of believability very high and would certainly raise issues pertaining to evidence and proof. However, the goal of strategic disinformation campaigns is usually more basic—and, paradoxically, simultaneously also more fundamental—

that is, destabilising the audience's the capacity to judge (Till, 2021, p. 12). That can be done either by increasing certainty and stubbornness in the target's attitudes by feeding them attitude-conforming information (in terms of articles, posts, comments etc.) if those attitudes are useful to the threat agent or, conversely, decreasing certainty if the present attitudes are unfavourable to the threat actor; the latter is achieved by intentionally pushing counter-attitudinal information, e.g. through mass-generated comments, so that members of the target audience start doubting themselves and, therefore, become politically incapacitated (Zerback et al., 2021, pp. 1083–1084). The latter are often carried out by way of simulating grassroots opinion—referred to, appropriately, as astroturfing after a type of artificial grass – flooding the public sphere with comments, posts, and other content by using fake accounts, both human-controlled and automated (Zerback et al., 2021, p. 1092). In this way, threat actors are able to engage in inauthentic agenda-setting by amplifying some messages (often fake or manipulated) and crowding out others (Ehrett et al., 2021).

Indeed, the main threat of fake news is less that they will convert those who encounter them into believing a specific conspiracy theory or propaganda narrative (although that can, and does, happen), but that they undermine 'the very fabric by which reasoned opinions can be formed, decisions can be made and consensus can be achieved' (Miller, 2020, p. 171). In other words, the aim is, typically, less about making everyone believe a single fakery than about making it unable what the criteria for truth are (let alone what truth itself is). Likewise, for Lewandowsky et al. (2017, p. 355), the very abundance of competing 'facts' has the effect of eroding trust in facts altogether.

As a result of the above characteristics, an increasing number of actors, including states, are willing to engage in what could be, in different contexts, called information operations, hostile social manipulation, or any other of a plethora of competing terms. Notably, Mazarr et al. (2019, p. 1), in their programmatic study for the RAND Corporation, define hostile social manipulation as '*the purposeful systematic generation and dissemination of information to produce harmful social, political, and economic outcomes in a target country by affecting beliefs, attitudes, and behavior*'. A typical technique, used by disinformation agents, is infiltration of discourse within partisan communities and capitalisation on pre-existing tensions by further exacerbating them (Bastos et al., 2021, p. 15), often through simultaneous building up of within-community pride and feel-good factor (e.g. in social media groups) and simultaneous informational and emotional alienation from the groups pitched as the enemy (Schick, 2020, pp. 64–65).

While, for example, Nadler et al. (2018) use the term 'weaponisation' for any employment of data-fuelled algorithmic content governance in any context to convince users without their knowledge, the focus here is more narrow and conventional: the use of online platforms and other content delivery infrastructures by state and non-state actors to inflict (informational) harm on another state or sub-state group. Nevertheless, one must also admit that the above lack of differentiation is not without sense either as the same techniques that drive marketing campaigns can also be employed for the purpose of political manipulation and information warfare (see e.g. Kalpokas, 2017). In particular, that is the case with the combination of dynamic disinformation made possible and scalable by the emergence of synthetic media and the ubiquity of digital platforms, thereby enabling precision-targeting of propaganda (Polyakova, 2018).

Perhaps most notably among state actors, for Russia, 'information confrontation' in the broad sense, entails 'the clash of national interests and ideas, where superiority is sought by targeting the adversary's information infrastructure'—an understanding that covers not only ordinary cyber warfare but also 'a significant psychological remit, whereby an actor attempts to affect informational resources [. . .] as well as the minds of the adversary's military personnel and population at large' (Hakala & Melnychuk, 2021, p. 5; see also Kalpokas, 2016; Kalpokas & Kalpokiene, 2021). Once that is achieved, the cognitive integrity of a society becomes a matter of strategic confrontation, with the latter being ever-present and continuous, without a defined battlespace (Hakala & Melnychuk, 2021, pp. 6–7). Indeed, it is this lack of conformity with established norms and laws of armed conflict, such as separation between conflict and piece, combatants and civilians, battlefield and areas not subjected to military action that makes such 'information confrontation' extremely difficult to both conceptualise and counter in Western military strategy. In Russia, meanwhile, this has allegedly 'become part and parcel of [. . .] strategic thinking in foreign policy' that allows for making use of the grey area between conflict and peace (Polyakova, 2018; see also Pynnöniemi, 2019, p. 216).

The aim is typically to achieve 'reflexive control', i.e. to affect the calculations of the adversary (by tampering with the information on which such calculations are being made and, hence, their perception of reality) so that the outcomes of such calculations are to the benefit of the initiator of such an operation (Till, 2021, p. 1367; see also Kalpokas, 2016; Adamsky, 2018; Pynnöniemi, 2019). Alternatively, the target can be pushed into a condition whereby calculations cannot be made at all due to conflicting information or cognitive confusion (Thornton & Miron, 2020, p. 17). In either case, promotion of the attacking state's strategic interests, through action or inaction of the target, is key (Adamsky 2018, p. 41). Moreover, it must be kept in mind that while in a traditional conflict the targets are typically relatively clear due to the distinction between combatants and non-combatants, in information operations the spectrum of targets is intentionally broad and includes 'individuals, organisations, governments and societies' in a continuous and comprehensive manner (Adamsky 2018, p. 41; see also Pynnöniemi, 2019, p. 216). Hence, sophisticated information warfare is a matter of persistence, of gradually undermining target societies, and not a blitzkrieg.

As such, the idea of information warfare is not new—the use of disinformation as part of a broader military strategy can be traced to Antiquity and perhaps even further back (Patersman & Hanley, 2020, p. 444). However, while traditionally it had been a weapon of secondary importance, one that accompanied physical warfare, now information operations themselves take centre stage with the purpose of affecting public opinion even (and perhaps especially) in absence of other forms of conflict; hence, one must nowadays talk of a novel battlefield—one populated by 'Twitterbots, false accounts, sockpuppets, trolls, and paid influencers' (Bastos et al., 2021, p. 2). The use of technology, and AI-enabled tools in particular, thus can be seen as a major strategic innovation that contributes the threat landscape (see e.g. Thornton & Miron, 2020, p. 16).

References

Ackland, R., & Gwynn, K. (2021). Truth and the dynamics of group diffusion on twitter. In R. Greifeneder et al. (Eds.), *The psychology of fake news: Accepting, sharing, and correcting misinformation* (pp. 27–46). Routledge.

Adamsky, D. (2018). From Moscow with coercion: Russian deterrence theory and strategic culture. *Journal of Strategic Studies, 41*(1-2), 33–60.

Ammerman, W. (2019). *The invisible brand: Marketing in the age of automation, big data, and machine learning.* McGraw-Hill.

Bastos, M., Mercea, D., & Goveia, F. (2021). Guy next door and implausibly attractive young women: The visual frames of social media propaganda. *New Media & Society.* https://doi.org/10.1177/1461

Benkler, Y., Faris, R., & Roberts, H. (2018). *Network propaganda: Manipulation, disinformation, and radicalization in American politics.* Oxford University Press.

Bozdag, C. (2020). Managing diverse online networks in the context of polarization: Understanding how we grow apart on and through social media. *Social Media + Society.* https://doi.org/10.1177/2056305120975713

Brotherton, R. (2020). *Bad news: Why we fall for fake news.* Bloomsbury.

Bruns, A. (2019). *Are filter bubbles real?* Polity Press.

Chambers, D. (2019). Emerging temporalities in the multiscreen home. *Media, Culture & Society.* https://doi.org/10.1177/0163443719867851

Chandler, D. (2019). What is at stake in the critique of big data? Reflections on Christian Fuchs' chapter. In D. Chandler & C. Fuchs (Eds.), *Digital objects, digital subjects: Interdisciplinary perspectives on capitalism, labour and politics in the age of big data* (pp. 73–79). University of Westminster Press.

Citton, Y. (2019). *Mediarchy.* Polity Press.

Cotter, K., Medeiros, M., Pak, C., & Thorson, K. (2021). 'Reach the right people: The politics of 'Interests' in Facebook's classification system for ad targeting. *Big Data & Society.* https://doi.org/10.1177/2053951721996046

Courtenay-Smith, N. (2018). *Stand out online.* Piatkus.

Dahlgren, P. (2018). Media, knowledge and trust: The deepening epistemic crisis of democracy. *Javnost – The Public, 25*(1), 20–27.

Doyle, W., & Roda, C. (2019). Introduction. In W. Doyle & C. Roda (Eds.), *Communication in the era of attention scarcity* (pp. 1–6). Palgrave Macmillan.

Ehrett, C., et al. (2021). Inauthentic news feeds and agenda setting in a coordinated inauthentic information operation. *Social Science Computer Review.* https://doi.org/10.1177/08944393211019951

Gil de Zúñiga, H., Weeks, B., & Ardèvol-Abreu, A. (2017). Effects of the news-finds-me perception in communication: social media use implications for news seeking and learning about politics. *Journal of Computer-Mediated Communication, 22*, 102–123.

Hakala, J., & Melnychuk, J. (2021). *Russia's Strategy in cyberspace.* NATO STRATCOM COE.

Harsin, J. (2019). Political attention: A genealogy of reinscriptions. In W. Doyle & C. Roda (Eds.), *Communication in the era of attention scarcity* (pp. 75–113). Palgrave Macmillan.

Hendricks, V. F., & Vestergaard, M. (2019). *Reality lost: Markets of attention, misinformation and manipulation.* Springer.

Hepp, A., Breiter, A., & Hasebrink, U. (2018). Rethinking transforming communications: An introduction. In A. Hepp, A. Breiter, & U. Hasebrink (Eds.), *Communicative figurations: Transformative communications in times of deep mediatization* (pp. 3–13). Palgrave Macmillan.

Hermann, E. (2021). Artificial intelligence and mass personalisation of communication content: An ethical and literacy perspective. *New Media & Society.* https://doi.org/10.1177/14614448211022702

Jankowicz, N. (2020). *How to lose the information war: Russia, fake news, and the future of conflict.* I.B. Tauris.

Kalpokas, I. (2016). Social media: Mimesis and warfare. *Lithuanian Foreign Policy Review, 35,* 116–133.

Kalpokas, I. (2017). Information warfare on social media: A brand management perspective. *Baltic Journal of Law and Politics, 10*(1), 35–62.

Kalpokas, I. (2018). *A political theory of post-truth.* Palgrave Macmillan.

Kalpokas, I., & Kalpokiene, J. (2021). Synthetic media and information warfare: Assessing potential threats. In H. Mölder, V. Sazonov, A. Chochia, & T. Kerikmäe (Eds.), *The Russian Federation in the global knowledge warfare.* Springer.

Kormelink, T. G., & Meijer, I. C. (2019). Material and sensory dimensions of everyday news use. *Media, Culture & Society, 41*(5), 637–653.

Kryston, K., & Eden, A. (2021). I like what you like: Social norms and media enjoyment. *Mass Communication and Society.* https://doi.org/10.1080/15205436.2021.1934703

Lewandowsky, S., Ecker, U. K. H., & Cook, J. (2017). Beyond misinformation: Understanding and coping with the 'Post-truth' era. *Journal of Applied Research in Memory and Cognition, 16*(4), 353–369.

Libicki, M. C. (2017). The convergence of information warfare. *Strategic Studies Quarterly, 11*(1), 49–65.

Maddalena, G., & Gili, G. (2020). *The history and theory of post-truth communication.* Palgrave Macmillan.

Mazarr, M. J., Bauer, R. M., Casey, A., Heintz, S. A., & Matthews, L. J. (2019). *The emerging risk of virtual societal warfare: Social manipulation in a changing information environment.* The RAND Corporation.

Miller, V. (2020). *Understanding digital culture* (2nd ed.). SAGE Publications.

Nadler, A., Crain, M., & Donovan, J. (2018). *Weaponizing the digital influence machine.* Data & Society Research Institute, https://datasociety.net/wp-content/uploads/2018/10/DS_Digital_Influence_Machine.pdf

O'Shaughnessy, N. (2020). From disinformation to fake news: Forwards into the past. In P. Baines, N. O'Shaughnessy, & N. Snow (Eds.), *The SAGE handbook of propaganda* (pp. 55–70). SAGE.

Palano, D. (2019). The truth in a bubble: The end of 'Audience Democracy' and the rise of 'Bubble Democracy'. *Soft Power, 6*(2), 37–53.

Patersman, T., & Hanley, L. (2020). Political warfare in the digital age: Cyber subversion, information operations and 'Deep Fakes'. *Australian Journal of International Affairs, 74*(4), 439–454.

Polyakova, A. (2018, November 15). Weapons of the Weak: Russia and AI-driven Asymmetric Warfare. *The Brookings Institution,* https://www.brookings.edu/research/weapons-of-the-weak-russia-and-ai-driven-asymmetric-warfare/

Pomerantsev, P. (2019). *This is not propaganda: Adventures in the war against reality.* Faber & Faber.

Pynnöniemi, K. (2019). Information-psychological warfare in Russian security strategy. In R. E. Kanet (Ed.), *Routledge handbook of Russian security* (pp. 214–226). Routledge.

Schick, N. (2020). *Deep fakes and the infocalypse: What you urgently need to know.* Monoray.

Schwartz, N., & Jalbert, M. (2021). When (Fake) news feels true: Intuitions of truth and correction of misinformation. In R. Greifeneder et al. (Eds.), *The psychology of fake news: Accepting, sharing, and correcting misinformation* (pp. 74–89). Routledge.

Seubert, S., & Becker, C. (2019). The culture industry revisited: Sociophilosophical reflections on 'Privacy' in the digital age. *Philosophy and Social Criticism, 45*(8), 930–947.

Shmargad, Y., & Klar, S. (2020). Sorting the news: How ranking by popularity polarizes our politics. *Political Communication, 37*(3), 423–446.

Strauß, N., Huber, B., & Gil de Zúñiga, H. (2021). Structural influences on the news finds me perception: Why people believe they don't have to actively seek news anymore. *Social Media + Society.* https://doi.org/10.1177/20563051211024966

Sunstein, C. R. (2018). *#Republic*. Princeton University Press.

Syvertsen, T. (2020). *Digital detox: The politics of disconnecting*. Emerald Publishing.

Thornton, R., & Miron, M. (2020). Toward the 'Third Revolution in Military Affairs': The Russian military's use of ai-enabled cyber warfare. *The RUSI Journal, 165*(3), 12–21.

Till, C. (2021). Propaganda through 'Reflexive Control' and the mediated construction of reality. *New Media & Society, 23*(6), 1362–1378.

Vaidhyanathan, S. (2018). *Anti-social media: How facebook disconnects us and undermines democracy*. Oxford University Press.

van Dijck, J., Poell, T., & de Waal, M. (2018). *The platform society: Public values in a connective World*. Oxford University Press.

Wanless, A., & Berk, M. (2020). The audience is the amplifier: Participatory propaganda. In P. Baines, N. O'Shaughnessy, & N. Snow (Eds.), *The SAGE handbook of propaganda* (pp. 85–104). SAGE.

Woolley, S. C., & Guilbeault, D. R. (2017). Computational propaganda in the United States of America: Manufacturing consensus online. *Oxford Internet Institute Working Paper No.* 2017.5.

Zamith, R., Belair-Gagnon, V., & Lewis, S. C. (2020). Constructing audience quantification: Social influences and the development of norms about audience analytics and metrics. *New Media & Society, 22*(10), 1763–1764.

Zerback, T., Töpfl, F., & Knöpfle, M. (2021). The disconcerting potential of online disinformation: Persuasive effects of astroturfing comments and three strategies of inoculation against them. *New Media & Society, 23*(5), 1080–1098.

Zuboff, S. (2019). *The age of surveillance capitalism: The fight for a human future at the new frontier of power*. Profile Books.

Chapter 3
On Human Susceptibility: Assessing Potential Threats

In an already attention-intensive environment characterised by 'chaos and disorder' as well as 'a blurring of work and home zones, spurred by notions of temporal excess, absorption, immersion and a squandering of time' (Chambers, 2019, p. 3), it comes as no surprise that individuals aim to minimise their cognitive load whenever possible. Indeed, according to the cognitive bottleneck theory, even when as few as two cognitive tasks need to be performed simultaneously, there will already be 'a decrease in performance in at least one of the tasks', necessitating a strategic balancing and distribution of attention (Tanner, 2020, p. 66; an identical point, albeit expressed in different terms, is also stressed by Citton, 2017, pp. 31–32 as well as Hendricks & Vestergaard, 2019, p. 3). Notably, information acquisition transpires to be one such area where savings are being made. It is, therefore, not accidental that this juncture of object selection and attention allocation is exactly the weak spot that disinformation agents increasingly seem to target (Till, 2021, pp. 1364–1365). Under such circumstances, reliance on substitutes to cognition, such as 'emotional cues, experience, and existing beliefs' ultimately 'saves time and cognitive energy and leads to quicker but more biased decisions than using rational cues' (Park & Kaye, 2019, p. 6; see also Kim, 2018, p. 4819). In this way, fake content already has as advantage in the very fact that it can be manufactured and refashioned in any way that the audience will find appealing.

The importance of first impressions is also demonstrated by sharing behaviour on social media: studies suggest that around half of the stories shared on social media had not even been read by the user (Schwartz & Jalbert, 2021, p. 74; see also Gabielkov et al., 2016). In fact, even trivial details, such as the font and colour of the text, the quality of the visuals etc. count as they affect the ease of access and the time and effort necessary for processing (Schwartz & Jalbert, 2021, pp. 79–80). Moreover, details such as adding even a random, vaguely (if at all) associative photo to a text will increase its uptake regardless of other attributes, such as veracity, by simply making the content seem more familiar and more easily retrievable from memory (Newman & Zhang, 2021). Hence, initial, primarily intuitive assessment of (perceived) trustworthiness becomes the key gatekeeping tool for individuals

I. Kalpokas, J. Kalpokiene, *Deepfakes*, SpringerBriefs in Political Science, https://doi.org/10.1007/978-3-030-93802-4_3

(Schwartz & Jalbert, 2021, p. 74). Notably, a related tendency is that the more users feel overwhelmed with content, the less effort they are willing to put into parsing through it (Park, 2019, p. 8). That only serves to illustrate that the bar of quality and truthlikeness necessary for content to gain traction might not even be particularly high.

Spoilt by both choice and an environment in which potentially any information may or may not be correct, 'users tend to engage with content that brings cognitive benefits but does not require extensive cognitive effort', typically opting for content that manifests 'novelty [. . .] and digestibitily' (Noon Nave et al., 2018, p. 3). Indeed, as people are inundated with information, they start lacking the time, cognitive, and motivational resources to thoroughly and effectively comprehend the situation, making them ask 'how does this fit in with what I already believe' (Ecker, 2018, p. 80). This tendency to search for opinion-congruence provides a psychological backdrop to the formation of online groups and communities united by shared patterns of information consumption. Indeed, as stressed by O'Shaughnessy (2020, p. 64), '[d]isinformation is effective because it energises confirmation bias, that is, the tendency of new information to merely entrench further the fault lines of existing perspectives', particularly in situations where individuals are primarily interacting with the like-minded (see also e.g. Post, 2019, p. 10). Likewise, for Schwartz and Jalbert (2021, p. 75), 'a claim is more likely to be accepted as true when it is *compatible* with other things one knows'. Indeed, time and time again, individuals manifest a 'desire to believe' in order to have their view of the world confirmed (Maddalena & Gili, 2020, p. 90). That is particularly the case in contexts where the media environment is fragmented, thus enabling even more opportunities to find and choose something that is opinion-congruent (Steppat et al., 2021, p. 2). Indeed, it is by now uncontroversial that 'opinion-congruent information is rapidly and involuntarily associated with truthfulness' and vice versa as 'people involuntarily reject factual propositions that conflict with their knowledge of the world' while uncritically accepting opinion-congruent ones (Gilead et al., 2019, p. 399).

Moreover, since widely-held understandings of fake news typically manifest a strong first-person-centricity (it is never 'me' or 'us' who believe in and share fake news but 'them'), getting individuals change their news consumption behaviours is notoriously difficult (Lyons et al., 2021, pp. 13–14). Hence, anything that is threatening to 'our' widely-held views must be merely fake news perpetuated by 'them' (Axt et al., 2021, p. 223). The latter also extends to an oversensitivity about the protection of the in-group, even from imaginary threats to its integrity, value or other shared attributes; hence, the identity-based good 'us' versus bad 'them' information filtering is to be seen as both powerful and pervasive (Oysterman & Dawson, 2021). Consequently, it should come as no surprise that 'factchecks not only fail to correct falsehoods, they often cause individuals to double down on incorrect information' (Jankowicz, 2020, p. 202). Still, some caution might be necessary: as Sunstein (2018, p. 17) observes, 'Filtering is inevitable, a fact of life. It is as old as humanity itself. It is built into our minds. No human being can see, hear, or read everything' leading humans to constantly filter out information in order to make their environment manageable. However, problems do arise when threat actors manage to hijack this filtering process.

Hilbert (2020), meanwhile, is even more straightforward when asserting that 'to get our attention hooked to the screen, algorithms simply need to get us at our worst: our narcissism, vanity, gullibility, our non-negotiable righteousness, our anger, envy, lust, and greed'. Nevertheless, one should perhaps be less dismissive – after all, the human brain appears to have evolved as a problem-solving tool rather than an information storage facility and, therefore, ignorance might simply be inevitable, particularly if illusions can serve solving the challenge at hand (such as making a political choice) more efficiently than factual information (Sloman & Fernbach, 2017). As a useful addition to the preceding, Margolin (2020) formulates a theory of informative fictions. According to this approach, fake information might be perceived as effectively more true than truth itself by revealing expected or suspected traits, attributes, motivations, and character of individuals (such as politicians), events, or developments. For this reason, inaccurate (or outrightly fictitious) content can be tolerated and even embraced if it is seen to underscore or demonstrate an underlying 'truth' (Margolin, 2020, p. 2). Particularly as 'issues of concern' to a particular audience and ways of approaching them can be identified in advance with high fidelity and response to messaging can be monitored (e.g. through sentiment analysis) in order to either tweak or weigh in on a particular narrative depending on its performance, the capacity to tap into biases and pre-existing perspectives can be relatively easily maximised (Wanless & Berk, 2020, p. 88).

Clearly, then, the likelihood of the uptake of claims is conditional not only on their truth-likeness (in terms of the quality of both content and its presentation) but also on how they perform in a broader narrative that gives sense to disparate occurrences: as stressed by Baron (2018, p. 73), 'what matters to win a referendum or an election is not evidence (i.e. facts) but *meaning*'. Indeed, if a story lends coherence to the otherwise disparate parts, there is a higher likelihood of acceptance (Schwartz & Jalbert, 2021, p. 75). In fact, due to the importance of meaning and coherence, 'we do not store information verbatim, we seldom remember the exact wording of conversations of other communications'; therefore, we will subconsciously modify any content we encounter for it to fit pre-existing schemas and expectations of what the story should entail and what meaning it should convey (Marsh & Stanley, 2021, p. 135). Once people are 'transported into' a story—i.e. they feel like participants in an unfolding narrative with which they can easily identify and see themselves within—there is an increased likelihood that they will 'accept and internalize the attitudes, emotions, and representations of reality offered by the narrative' (McLaughlin & Velez, 2019, p. 25). Again, the flexibility of human cognition is simultaneously a tool for maintenance of continuity and meaning *and* a quality that can be hijacked for manipulative purposes.

Crucially, people seem to possess an innate 'desire to be "swept away" by a story world'—so much so that 'people are willing to lower the cognitive mechanisms they employ when critically evaluating persuasive information' in order to facilitate transportation into a story world they find appealing (McLaughlin & Velez, 2019, p. 32). In this sense, even a poorly-constructed fake news story would find strong adherence within the target audience if it weaves into an already accepted broader story about the flawed character of the person in question or the institution that they represent. Indeed, tapping into the stories that are already floating around must be seen as an effective strategy. Crucially, humans are model-making creatures, and it is always much more comfortable to have one's model complete; for that reason, audiences are often 'willing to accept information that is maybe not very reliable or valid' as long as such information 'allows them to build complete models of the world so they have what feels like a complete understanding' (Ecker, 2018, p. 80). A similar perspective, with a particular emphasis on strategic communications, is also provided by Holmstrom (2015, pp. 120–121) who asserts, in no uncertain terms, that people need a narrative because it 'provides explanations', i.e. 'describes the past, justifies the present, and presents a vision of the future', while '[m]ore and more pure information or facts only muddles our understanding of the world', increasing the desire for clear-cut stories. Likewise, as Kim (2018, p. 4808) contends, since 'humans have a core social motive to comprehend the situations and act effectively, they try to resolve uncertainty when the meaning or the impact of situations is unclear' even if that involves reliance on rumour or other unverified or unreliable information. To that extent, people effectively *demand* to be deceived as they actively seek out information that falls in line with existing preconceptions or aligns with clearly identifiable and consumable patterns/narratives (Woolley & Joseff, 2020, p. 6).

No less importantly, a key factor affecting the political behaviour of citizens is not actually *being* informed but, instead, the *perception* of being informed: as this perception increases self-assessed political efficacy, such users 'may play an active role in democracy despite their illusion of being informed' (Song et al., 2020, p. 64). Likewise, the more users become used to simply encountering information through-out their daily (social) media routines, the less they are willing to keep themselves informed intentionally by seeking out news (Park & Kaye, 2020, p. 16). There are, of course, considerable efficiencies as no more need is felt to put effort into finding information that is of interest. At the same time, though, we are dependent on the information that we encounter, and such encounters are typically structured in accordance with our data profiles, increasingly isolating us from those who have generated different data (Ammerman, 2019, p. 36). That, in turn, allows for a multi-stage model of disinformation, whereby audiences are first primed for a particular type of disinformation, e.g. by cultivating certain attitudes and emotions, to only subsequently be targeted with the actual message (Woolley & Joseff, 2020, p. 23). The data necessary for threat actors typically comes from multiple streams, such as 'user data they legally buy from data brokers, illegal data they purchase from hackers, and data they retrieve themselves' (Paul & Posard, 2020). In this way, truly smart targeting of disinformation is made possible, essentially trapping target audiences within content that they cannot but believe in.

The scheme for the above narrowing of information horizons is not just the result of malevolent practices by threat actors but also significantly aided and abetted by algorithmic governance processes, particularly on social media platforms: as every positive reaction to a given content type is recorded, similar content is pushed to the users in question, and as these users see more of the same, they also share more of the same, thereby affecting their broader networks (Singer & Brooking, 2019, p. 123). The groups and communities thereby formed effectively become crucial points of reference as well as sources of identity and attachment, not least because they offer the security and guaranteed affirmation that comes from speaking to one's own cohort (Davies, 2019, p. 177; O'Shaughnessy, 2020, p. 64). And if content, regardless of its veracity, taps into the predominant moods of such reference networks, particularly in the absence of countervailing information, it is likely to become eminently more believable regardless of any other attributes. Such self-referentiality has also led to 'the diminishing importance of anchoring political utterances in relation to verifiable facts' (Hopkin & Rosamond, 2018, p. 642), whence what matters is not whether the uttered things are true but whether the audience would *like* these things to be true (Lockie, 2016).

In the above context, truth becomes 'simply a matter of assertion' (Suiter, 2016, p. 27) or simply 'beside the point' (Vaidhyanathan 2018, p. 13). To that effect, one must agree with Ammerman (2019, p. 37) in stating that '[w]e have shifted from consuming information we need, to consuming information we like', particularly with regards to our propensity for seeking out bias-congruent information (Woolley & Joseff, 2020, p. 6), meaning that there is a market demand for deception. After all, it must be remembered that misperceptions, particularly if they fit pre-existing views, are often more comfortable to embrace (Strong, 2017, p. 140) than factual, but opinion-incongruent information, thereby giving palatable disinformation a clear competitive advantage (O'Shaughnessy, 2020, p. 64). Hence, it should come as no surprise whatsoever that the information environment has become the battlefield it is today, even in absence of advanced content generation techniques, such as synthetic media and deepfakes in particular.

Crucially, the tendency to opt for opinion-congruent information appears to also be hardwired in human physiology: the confirmation that we receive, however imaginary, stimulates the release of pleasure hormones, which then translate into positive changes in bodily characteristics, such as blood pressure or muscle tension (Damasio, 2018). Such stimulation, and our craving for it, clearly opens door for manipulation: as Ammerman (2019, p. 51) notes, 'we all seek out pleasurable stimulation to our brain chemistry, and the rewards we receive from these chemicals, therefore, can be a prime way for someone to persuade us' (for a similar point, see also Mazarr et al., 2019, p. 52). Here it also must be kept in mind that with the ever-growing data footprint being left by users, the ever-increasing array of means of data collection, and rapid advances in affective computing, studying online sentiments and emotions has become both increasingly prevalent and increasingly scientific in methods and accuracy (Davies, 2019, p. 12), allowing data-rich actors to determine in advance the types of messaging (including fake content) that we are going to find pleasurable. Hence, target audiences are likely to find themselves in situations of little choice other than succumbing to the hardly resistible pleasure of being deceived (see e.g. Kalpokas, 2018; Kalpokas, 2020).

Here we can witness something similar to Eyal's (2019) model of hooking users through a continuous loop of trigger, action, variable reward, and investment. The trigger might be a prompt, such as the activation of a pre-known emotional propensity, intended to induce action, i.e. engagement with content in anticipation of a reward, such as (imaginary) confirmation of one's attitudes, opinions, and predilections; crucially, it transpires that even the expectation of a reward already causes a surge in pleasure hormones (Eyal, 2019, p. 8). In fact, it is this expectation that constitutes the most exciting phase, while the actual reward must be sufficient to retain interest, but not always maximised so as not to become predictable and boring. Finally, the investment phase is where user retention is sealed: as users invest their time and effort (reading, watching, commenting) and reputation (liking, sharing), the cost of abandoning the source or admitting (even to oneself) to having fallen prey to manipulation becomes very high (for a fuller elaboration of this model, albeit focused on app design, see Eyal, 2019, pp. 7–10). In this way, the expectation of satisfaction to be offered by content (for example, because similar content has been pleasurable in the past or because a particular source is already associated with pleasure) is already enough to attract attention, and if investment is made in the form of engagement, there seemingly remains no way back.

No less importantly, virality metrics (the number of likes, shares, views etc.) can be perceived as a good enough indication of the attention-worthiness of content, thereby increasing the urge for interaction (Kim, 2018, p. 4811). In the social media environment overloaded with stimuli, 'it is natural to seek mental shortcuts for evaluating unfamiliar information'; hence, virality metrics can easily trigger bandwagoning, i.e. the perception that if many people see an item as valuable, then it simply *must* be valuable (Kim, 2018, p. 4819). Likewise, for Hannan (2018, p. 220), not only '[p]opularity now competes with logic and evidence as an arbiter of truth' but, in fact, 'popularity often carries more persuasive power than the appeal to impersonal fact'. The problem here is not only that there is no necessary relationship between popularity and veracity (and if there is, the indications are that veracity is likely to be negatively associated with popularity) but also that it is easy to manipulate popularity metrics through simulated social media engagement (Woollacott, 2019). In other cases, this energy and time-saving function is performed by less quantifiable cues, such as emotion and experience that produce a seemingly intuitive fit with particular content (Park & Kaye, 2019, p. 6). In this way, even manifestly fake content is likely to be attractive to audiences in the characteristic 'famous for being famous' kind of way as long as it generates a critical mass of initial attention and traction.

Simultaneously, there is even evidence that the more people are (or feel) overwhelmed with news, the less effort they put into actually reading them, to the extent that some even start avoiding news consumption altogether (Park, 2019, p. 8), thereby further inflating the power of the pieces of information that actually *do* break through. Ultimately, what the threat actors achieve if they manage to cut through this avoidance is a near-monopoly of decision-making resources, achieving 'reflexive control' over their audiences and disrupting the ability of the latter 'to make judgements in their own interests' (Till, 2021, p. 12). In this context, a useful strategy (on the manipulator's side, of course) once again involves opting for emotions, particularly as emotional content transpires to gain more traction (Park & Kaye,

2019, p. 6). No less pertinently, even conventional news reporting seems to be increasingly moving towards the affective register (Papacharissi, 2019, p. 2). In fact, as Song and Xu (2019, p. 6) demonstrate, emotions themselves can be seen as social information because '[e]xpressing emotion permits group members to convey information about their appraisal of a situation' and may also 'elicit affective reactions and/or cognitive inferences in others, which enables rapid social coordination'. Unsurprisingly, users are particularly likely to share content which is 'emotionally provocative'; however, not any such provocation will fare equally well, since '[i] nformation that evokes high-arousal emotions like fear, disgust, awe, and anger is shared more than information that stimulates low-arousal emotions like sadness' (Woolley & Joseff, 2020, p. 7). Similarly, as Jaffé and Greifeneder (2021) show, negatively framed statements are more likely to be judged as true than those conveying the same message but framed positively (i.e. we are more likely to believe that the glass is half-empty than that it is half-full). In such situations, audiences are likely to pay attention to—and interact with—content not for its *informational* value but for the *emotional* valence of a particular item, again putting veracity in the back seat.

There are, however, more applications of disinformation than influence operations aiming to change a population's attitudes on a large scale. Disinformation is often also used to discredit opposition, not only in the form of direct political competitors but, even more ominously, opposition activists. Here even lower-grade fake news can be effective as the burden of verisimilitude necessary to discredit a private person (or, at least, to cause enough distress to serve as a deterrent) is likely lower than one necessary to discredit a major political figure. That is particularly dangerous in a world in which political leaders do not shy away from mobilising cyber-militias and social media mobs with the aim of smearing, harassing, and intimidating dissenters into silence and submission or undermining their reputation sufficiently for them not to be listened to (Pomerantsev, 2019, p. 41), either outcome being particularly traumatic in a 'culture of compulsory digital sociality' (Kuntsman & Miyake, 2019, p. 909). As will be shown in the subsequent chapters, deepfakes in can add yet another, and particularly distressing, dimension to such discrediting and harassment efforts. Moreover, as should be clear from this chapter, deepfakes do not even need to be fully convincing to achieve their aim—they only must be placed in a susceptible environment.

References

Ammerman, W. (2019). *The invisible brand: Marketing in the age of automation, big data, and machine learning*. McGraw-Hill.

Axt, J. R., Landau, M. J., & Kay, A. C. (2021). Fake news attributions as a source of nonspecific structure. In R. Greifeneder et al. (Eds.), *The psychology of fake news: Accepting, sharing, and correcting misinformation* (pp. 220–234). Routledge.

Baron, I. Z. (2018). *How to save politics in a post-truth era*. Manchester University Press.

Chambers, D. (2019). Emerging temporalities in the multiscreen home. *Media, Culture & Society*. https://doi.org/10.1177/0163443719867851

Citton, Y. (2017). *The ecology of attention*. Polity.

Damasio, A. (2018). *The strange order of things: Life, feeling, and the making of cultures*. Pantheon Books.

Davies, W. (2019). *Nervous states: How feeling took over the World*. Vintage.

Ecker, U. K. H. (2018). Why rebuttals may not work: The psychology of misinformation. *Media Asia, 44*(2), 79–87.

Eyal, N. (2019). *Hooked: How to build habit-forming products*. Penguin.

Gabielkov, M., Ramachandran, A., Chaintreau, A., & Legout, A. (2016). Social clicks: What and who gets read on twitter. *Performance Evaluation Review, 44*, 179–192.

Gilead, M., Sela, M., & Maril, A. (2019). That's my truth: Evidence for involuntary opinion confirmation. *Social Psychological and Personality Science, 10*(3), 393–401.

Hannan, J. (2018). Trolling ourselves to death? Social media and post-truth politics. *European Journal of Communication, 33*(2), 214–226.

Hendricks, V. F., & Vestergaard, M. (2019). *Reality lost: Markets of attention, misinformation and manipulation*. Springer.

Hilbert, M. (2020, April 25). Social media distancing: An opportunity to debug our relationship with out algorithms. *Medium*, https://medium.com/@martinhilbert/social-media-distancing-an-opportunity-to-debug-our-relationship-with-our-algorithms-a64889c0b1fc

Holmstrom, M. (2015). The narrative and social media. *Defence Strategic Communications, 1*(1), 119–133.

Hopkin, J., & Rosamond, B. (2018). Post-truth politics, bullshit and bad ideas: 'Deficit Fetishism' in the UK. *New Political Economy, 23*(6), 641–655.

Jaffé, M. E., & Greifeneder, R. (2021). Can that be true or is it just fake news? New perspectives on the negativity bias in judgments of truth. In R. Greifeneder et al. (Eds.), *The psychology of fake news: Accepting, sharing, and correcting misinformation* (pp. 115–130). Routledge.

Jankowicz, N. (2020). *How to lose the information war: Russia, fake news, and the future of conflict*. I.B. Tauris.

Kalpokas, I. (2018). *A political theory of post-truth*. Palgrave Macmillan.

Kalpokas, I. (2020). Post-truth and the changing information environment. In N. O'Shaughnessy, N. Snow, & P. Baines (Eds.), *The SAGE handbook of propaganda* (pp. 71–84). SAGE.

Kim, J. W. (2018). Rumor has it: The effects of virality metrics in rumor believability and transmission on twitter. *New Media & Society, 20*(2), 4807–4825.

Kuntsman, A., & Miyake, E. (2019). The paradox and continuum of digital disengagement: Denaturalising digital sociality and technological connectivity. *Media, Culture & Society, 41*(6), 901–913.

Lockie, S. (2016). Post-truth politics and the social sciences. *Environmental Sociology, 2*(3), 233–237.

Lyons, B. A., Merola, V., & Reifler, J. (2021). How bad is the fake news problem? The role of baseline information in public perceptions. In R. Greifeneder et al. (Eds.), *The psychology of fake news: Accepting, sharing, and correcting misinformation* (pp. 11–26). Routledge.

Maddalena, G., & Gili, G. (2020). *The history and theory of post-truth communication*. Palgrave Macmillan.

Margolin, D. B. (2020). The theory of informative fictions: A character-based approach to false news and other misinformation. *Communication Theory*. https://doi.org/10.1093/ct/qtaa002

Marsh, E. J., & Stanley, M. L. (2021). False beliefs: Byproducts of an adaptive knowledge base? In R. Greifeneder et al. (Eds.), *The psychology of fake news: Accepting, sharing, and correcting misinformation* (pp. 131–146). Routledge.

Mazarr, M. J., Bauer, R. M., Casey, A., Heintz, S. A., & Matthews, L. J. (2019). *The emerging risk of virtual societal warfare: Social manipulation in a changing information environment*. The RAND Corporation.

McLaughlin, B., & Velez, J. A. (2019). Imagined politics: How different media platforms transport citizens into political narratives. *Social Science Computer Review, 37*(1), 22–37.

Newman, E. J., & Zhang, L. (2021). Truthiness: How non-probative photos shape belief. In R. Greifeneder et al. (Eds.), *The psychology of fake news: Accepting, sharing, and correcting misinformation* (pp. 90–114). Routledge.

Noon Nave, N., Shifman, L., & Tenenboim-Weinblatt, K. (2018). Talking it personally: Features of successful political posts on facebook. *Social Media + Society*. https://doi.org/10.1177/2056305118784771

O'Shaughnessy, N. (2020). From disinformation to fake news: Forwards into the past. In P. Baines, N. O'Shaughnessy, & N. Snow (Eds.), *The SAGE handbook of propaganda* (pp. 55–70). SAGE.

Oysterman, D., & Dawson, A. (2021). Your fake news, our facts: Identity-based motivation shapes what we believe, share, and accept. In R. Greifeneder et al. (Eds.), *The psychology of fake news: Accepting, sharing, and correcting misinformation* (pp. 173–195). Routledge.

Papacharissi, Z. (2019). Forget Messiahs. *Social Media + Society*. https://doi.org/10.1177/2056305119849710

Park, C. S. (2019). Does too much news on social media discourage news seeking? Mediating role of news efficacy between perceived news overload and news avoidance on social media. *Social Media + Society*. https://doi.org/10.1177/2056305119872956

Park, C. S., & Kaye, B. K. (2019). Expanding visibility on twitter: author and message characteristics and retweeting. *Social Media + Society*. https://doi.org/10.1177/2056305119834595

Park, C. S., & Kaye, B. K. (2020). What's this? Incidental exposure to news on social media, news-finds-me perception, news efficacy, and news consumption. *Mass Communication and Society, 23*(2), 157–180.

Paul, C., & Posard, M. N. (2020). Artificial intelligence and the manufacturing of reality. *The RAND Blog*, https://www.rand.org/blog/2020/01/artificial-intelligence-and-the-manufacturing-of-reality.html

Pomerantsev, P. (2019). *This is not propaganda: Adventures in the war against reality*. Faber & Faber.

Post, S. (2019). Polarizing communication as media effects on antagonists. Understanding communication in conflicts in digital media societies. *Communication Theory, 29*(2), 213–235.

Schwartz, N., & Jalbert, M. (2021). When (Fake) news feels true: Intuitions of truth and correction of misinformation. In R. Greifeneder et al. (Eds.), *The psychology of fake news: Accepting, sharing, and correcting misinformation* (pp. 74–89). Routledge.

Singer, P. W., & Brooking, E. T. (2019). *Like war: The weaponization of social media*. Mariner Books.

Sloman, S., & Fernbach, P. (2017). *The knowledge illusion: Why we never think alone*. Riverhead Books.

Song, H. G., de Zúñiga, H., & Boomgarden, H. G. (2020). Social media news use and political cynicism: Differential pathways through "News Finds Me" perception. *Mass Communication and Society, 23*(1), 47–70.

Song, Y., & Xu, R. (2019). Affective ties that bind: Investigating the affordances of social networking sites for commemoration of traumatic events. *Social Science Computer Review, 37*(3), 333–354.

Steppat, D., Castro Herrero, L., & Esser, F. (2021). Selective exposure in different political information environments: How media fragmentation and polarization shape congruent news use. *European Journal of Communication*. https://doi.org/10.1177/02673231211012141

Strong, S. I. (2017). Alternative facts and the post-truth society: Meeting the challenge. *University of Pennsylvania Law Review, 165*, 137–146.

Suiter, J. (2016). Post-truth politics. *Political Insight, 7*(3), 25–27.

Sunstein, C. R. (2018). *#Republic*. Princeton University Press.

Tanner, S. (2020). *Delivering impact with digital resources: Planning strategy in the attention economy*. Facet Publishing.

Till, C. (2021). Propaganda through 'reflexive control' and the mediated construction of reality. *New Media and Society, 23*(6), 1367–1378.

Vaidhyanathan, S. (2018). *Anti-social media: How Facebook disconnects us and undermines democracy.* Oxford University Press.

Wanless, A., & Berk, M. (2020). The audience is the amplifier: Participatory propaganda. In P. Baines, N. O'Shaughnessy, & N. Snow (Eds.), *The SAGE handbook of propaganda* (pp. 85–104). SAGE.

Woollacott, E. (2019, December 6). Social Media platforms easy to manipulate, NATO Advisers Find. *Forbes*, https://www.forbes.com/sites/emmawoollacott/2019/12/06/youtube-is-easiest-platform-to-manipulate-nato-advisers-find/#742696333255

Woolley, S., & Joseff, K. (2020). *Demand for deceit: How the way we think drives disinformation.* National Endowment for Democracy and International Forum for Democratic Studies, https://www.ned.org/wp-content/uploads/2020/01/Demand-for-Deceit.pdf

Chapter 4
From GANs to Deepfakes: Getting the Characteristics Right

Broadly speaking, deepfakes can be defined within the intersection of technology and communication and/or visual representation as 'a technology that uses Artificial Intelligence to produce or edit contents of a video or an image to show something that never happened' (Young, 2019, p. 8). More precisely, as Whittaker et al. (2020, p. 92) note, 'deepfakes are the product of AI and the machine learning technique of "deep learning", which is used to train deep neural networks (DNNs)'; although composed of simple computational units, or artificial neurons, such networks are more than the sum total of their operations. Instead, 'when set up as a network of thousands and millions of units, these simple functions combine to perform complex feats, such as object recognition, language translation, or robot navigation' (Whittaker et al., 2020, p. 92). To further narrow things down, the creation process employs so-called Generative Adversarial Networks (GANs).

A GAN comprises of two artificial neural networks pitted against each other. The first of them, referred to as the generator, is tasked with creating fake video material, while the second one, referred to as the discriminator, is constantly probing the generator's output with the aim of finding faults. Once such faults are detected, the generator is able to learn from the detection, and thus generate a more truth-like output, while any such new creations only serve to improve the discriminator's detection capacities. Such competition, which only ceases when the discriminator is no longer capable of finding errors in the generated material, allows a GAN to learn from itself and improve its own capacities in the process (for a more detailed description, see e.g. Chesney & Citron, 2019, p. 148; Giles et al., 2019, p. 8; Kelleher, 2019, p. 235; Young, 2019, p. 10). A corollary of this capacity for learning and self-improvement is that deepfakes will always be as truth-like as possible, given the quality of input material and the resources available. The same internal logic can only mean that the technology itself is bound to improve, making it even more difficult to distinguish between truth and falsehood (Galston, 2020). While first developed for synthetic image generation, the technology was subsequently employed for video as well—after all, given that a video is, effectively, merely a

I. Kalpokas, J. Kalpokiene, *Deepfakes*, SpringerBriefs in Political Science,
https://doi.org/10.1007/978-3-030-93802-4_4

sequence of images, such a move was not even particularly complicated (Breen, 2021, pp. 136–137).

As a result of their competitive setup, GANs are able to produce 'high-resolution facial images of nonexistent people, to create images of imaginary breeds of dogs, to assist artists in their paintings, for example, by filling in colored details to line drawings'; crucially, therefore, 'the speciality of GANs is to generate entirely novel content that is strikingly similar to the original, real images of people and things' (Whittaker et al., 2020, p. 93). Moreover, since the competitive principle at the heart of GANs is '[a]kin to an arms race between money counterfeiters and the police, the generator improves if its generated fake image was detected as such'— and likewise for the discriminator that learns from both correct labellings *and* mislabellings (that is also the case with all deep learning neural networks—they improve *regardless* of the outcome); as a consequence, such a model 'leads to incremental improvements on both sides' (Whittaker et al., 2020, p. 93).

To provide more context on the matter, deep learning, as a machine learning technique, 'is inspired by the human brain and organizes the neural network into multiple layers, each layer using different levels of abstraction' (Siggelkow and Terwiesch 2019, p. 85). Indeed, deep learning can be seen as 'a leap forward' in neural network technology due to their complex architectures that combine a large number of layers and thus enable otherwise challenging computations (Bown, 2021, pp. 178–179). Instead of explicit programming, as Whittaker et al. (2020, p. 93) stress, 'the function of a whole network of units is determined by the pattern of its unit connections'; in order to achieve the desired mode of performance, 'the connection strengths between units are adjusted via training on large sets of example data'. This structure of tiers and interconnections allows the network to learn (and create) fine-grained distinctions by reinforcing some and downgrading other connections and pathways within the network—perfect for the complex information processing that is necessary for digital content generation. However, deep learning is also notoriously opaque: while machine learning models do differ with regards to their interpretability, deep learning is likely the most difficult to penetrate, again, due to the layered and interconnected way in which artificial neurons are connected; the complicating factors include the scale of the network and the distribution of representations (the content is spread across vast numbers of artificial neurons, each performing only one simple operation), and the fact that whatever data is being processed, ends up being transformed all the time as the constitutive bits travel through the network, the result being that it is 'incredibly difficult to interpret, understand, and therefore explain, how the network is using an input to make a decision' (Kelleher, 2019, pp. 245–246). The upside, though, is the 'ability to learn patterns, and association between patterns, by being shown examples instead of being explicitly programmed' (Boden 2018, p. 72). Crucially, such artificial neural networks 'have the uncanny property of self-organization from a random start. [. . .] The system starts from a random architecture (random weights and connections), and gradually adapts itself to perform the task required' (Boden 2018, p. 70), which is of benefit for open-ended tasks—and generating visual output is precisely such a task.

As Andrejevic (2020, p. 4) observes, 'artificial intelligence "robotizes" mental labor: it promises to augment of displace the human role in communication, information processing, and decision-making' but also, arguably, creativity (as will be further explored later in this book). As such it 'resuscitates the promise of automation in the mental sphere: to be faster, more efficient, and more powerful than humans' (Andrejevic 2020, p. 4). Indeed, it is the simplicity of creation that results from such automation, particularly when paired with the ever more datafied and digitally documented nature of most people's lives that will, it is feared, 'heighten the potential for them to be used for malicious purposes such as blackmail, intimidation, sabotage, harassment, defamation, revenge porn, identity theft, and bullying' (Whittaker et al., 2020, pp. 94–95), the actual potential of which is to be explored in the subsequent chapter.

In general, the range of manipulation-related applications of deepfakes is broad and includes, among other factors, attempts to 'depict politicians making statements they never made, insert celebrities into porn videos and show people committing crimes they didn't commit' (Greengard, 2019, p. 164). Hence, to quote Maddalena and Gili (2020, p. 16), '[w]hile fake news deals in some way with the content of messages, deepfakes create a simulacrum of the speaker', further extending the destabilisation of information: not just the content but also the source or the subject can be fake. Such misrepresentations of individuals and their character are likely to have the potential of allowing malicious actors to manipulate elections or affect socio-political processes more broadly. Such attempts might include faking outrageous statements against some core constituencies, insinuating bribery, *quid pro quo* propositions, marital infidelity, or any other illegal or embarrassing acts that could be reasonably expected to undermine a candidate's campaign or their entire career, particularly if immediate and straightforward debunking is not possible. Moreover, particularly in more volatile situations (for example, in presence of social or ethnic tensions), fake inflammatory statements could even incite violence or, at least, protests that, in addition to their human and economic cost, would also serve to further undermine political life: even cases short of actual physical conflict could be serious enough to paralyse the public sphere, eroding trust in institutions etc. (Woolley & Joseff, 2020, p. 23; see also Greengard, 2020, p. 18; Shane, 2020, p. 35). Likewise, deepfakes could be employed as a means of negatively affecting diplomatic relations or inciting conflicts among groups and communities across state borders (Galston, 2020). Crucially, as evident from the first part of this paper, in case of pre-existing tensions, the bar for believability is dropped lower as well.

Another possible use could involve, for example, fake representation of crowds at an election rally, thus creating a false impression of campaign momentum and boosting the candidate's profile while the original footage can be dismissed as mainstream media trying to undermine the campaign (Young, 2019, pp. 83–85). In other cases of campaign-related manipulation, GANs can also be applied to generate fake text that is human-like, thereby automating (and thus increasing the output of) trolling. The concern is that '[t]his new automated astroturfing could result in a massive scaling up of operations, generating an entire fake public to influence political decisions' (Giles et al., 2019, p. 11). This factor is further reinforced by the use of deepfake profile images to make fake accounts look more real than if stock or stolen photos were used (Martineu, 2019; Simonite, 2020; Whittaker et al., 2020, p. 95). After all, as 'humans are more persuaded by other humans, especially when we hear or see them', the advent of 'real-looking, -sounding, and -seeming AI tools' is menacingly likely to 'change the foundations of trust and the truth' (Woolley, 2020, p. 150). Moreover, these campaigns would likely be easier to carry out, not necessitating the impersonation of hight-profile figures who are constantly under scrutiny and who would likely invest money and effort into debunking deepfakes. Here, fake popularity or a fake barrage of criticism might be enough to nudge the less-strongly opinionated voters in the manipulator's preferred direction. In case of such deepfake astroturfing, since nobody is personally harmed by having their likeness (if not identity) stolen, the chances of fake content being noticed as such and, therefore, reported and removed are decreased.

Notably, deep astroturfing could also have uses beyond outright manipulation: sometimes locking the opposition out of discourse can be a good enough result. In fact, in more mainstream communication techniques, one can already witness a paradoxical situation whereby the means and expenditures designed for attention attraction ultimately only increase the cacophony of stimuli, thereby becoming *distractions*; it does, however, transpire that at least a proportion of this effort is primarily aimed precisely not at convincing and mobilising people, but at making it more difficult for the competitors to reach key audiences (Kaplan, 2019, p. 1956). As a result, even deepfakes with limited truthlikeness can serve an important function: polluting the infosphere with deepfakes so that others find it more difficult (and/or costly) to attract attention, thereby locking audiences in their default positions. And, since it has already been established that the important factor in determining audience decisions is not actually being informed, but the *feeling* of being informed, establishing a verbal buffer zone of competing claims and opinions and thus preventing competing coherent meaningful (and, therefore, easy to take up) narratives from breaking through to target audiences becomes a strategic advantage.

It must be admitted that the predominant use of deepfakes is the creation of fake pornographic videos by transposing the likeness of a celebrity or some other person (as in deepfake revenge porn) onto pornographic content (see e.g. Statt, 2018; Popova, 2020). However, this tendency is more likely to be determined by motivational, rather than capacity, constraints. On the other hand, it is not impossible for the domains of deepfake pornography and politics to merge, as the fake porn videos of Michelle Obama or Ivanka Trump shows (see e.g. Lee, 2018). There also has been a case involving a sex tape of debated authenticity involving a high-ranking Malaysian politician and another man; although to this day it is unclear if the video was manipulated or not, and if it was, whether it was actually a deepfake, as some sources suggest (Kikerpill 2020), potential for actual deepfakes (given their proven sex video potential) to be used against prominent societal and political figures is laid bare. Moreover, pornographic deepfakes have already be used to target journalists and activist celebrities (again, exclusively female) for taking a stance on issues of societal importance with the explicit aim of discrediting and silencing them (see e.g. Maddocks, 2020).

One should, however, beyond the porno-political nexus, because the typical lack of political and/or other society-wide manipulative intention should not detract from the scale of the problem. Some authors even claim that the relative exclusion of deepfake pornography (an actual and acute threat) for the sake of political deepfakes (potential and uncertain threat) itself reproduces the patriarchal power hierarchies and misogynistic thinking that motivates deepfake pornography (see e.g. Gosse & Burkell, 2020). Synthetic pornography is, after all, how deepfakes first caught public attention when word of the technology started spreading on Reddit (Breen, 2021, pp. 134–135; Wilkerson, 2021, p. 409) and still around 96% of deepfake content available online is of pornographic nature (Pradhan, 2020), attesting to the scale of the problem and, arguably, acting as 'a catalyst for greater gender inequality', not least by undermining women and reproducing toxic gender-based stereotypes and behaviours (European Parliamentary Research Service, 2021, p. 24). Indeed, great harm can also be caused to ordinary individuals as 'the increasing use of deepfakes is already giving harassers new ways to generate disturbing, highly targeted videos for dissemination online' (Shane, 2020, p. 35). Moreover, there are ample tools for harassment, such as 'undressing' apps that use deepfake technology to digitally 'remove' clothes from photos of dressed women (see e.g. Clahane, 2020; Kirchengast, 2020, p. 309).

Indeed, as Whittaker et al. (2020, p. 95) observe, '[d]eepfakes are the next sinister breed of revenge porn which can make everyone potential targets even if they have never taken explicit photographs or videos of themselves'. Crucially, it must be noted that the various 'undressing' apps that are currently available share an explicitly sexist nature in that they only work on women's bodies: uploading an image of a male would still return a result with a female body (Kirchengast, 2020, p. 311). It is not accidental, therefore, that experts are already warning of an 'epidemic' of deepfake pornography (Selbie & Williams, 2021; see also Burgess, 2020). One aspect here is, of course, the emotional trauma suffered by the victims; however, one must also keep in mind that such fake videos are often used for e.g. harassment, causing intentional reputational harm, or blackmail (see e.g. McPeak, 2021, p. 436). A significant problem is also that, similarly to other forms of non-consensual pornography, such pictures are extremely difficult, if at all possible, to remove once they have spread across the internet (see e.g. Amer et al., 2021). Others, however, arguing from a feminist standpoint, would criticise the focus of female victimisation and instead emphasise the opportunities and empowerment offered by *consensual* deepfake pornography, e.g. through apps that enable users to allow their likeness to be used by selected content creators (see e.g. Rafaghello et al., 2019).

However, deepfakes can not only be used for large-scale manufacturing and dissemination of disinformation or for (sexual) harassment but also for targeted attempts at scamming selected individuals. For example, deepfakes are already of concern to businesses as there have been occurrences of employees being tricked into thinking their superior was calling to e.g. transfer large sums of money to a foreign account (Bateman, 2020; Gow, 2021; Noone, 2021). Also, deepfakes can be used to undermine the reputations of organisations and brands by portraying their representatives as saying or doing outrageous, illegal, or hypocritical things or by manufacturing 'proof' of dubious practices while grassroots outrage could be simulated (or amplified) through the use of automated social media accounts that make used of deepfake profile pictures (Bateman, 2020; Whittaker et al., 2020, p. 96). A similar threat can be faced by politicians who can be deceived into believing that they are conversing with colleagues or foreign partners. In such cases, deepfakes can be seen as attacks against the personal and professional credibility of those who are scammed (see e.g. The Baltic Times, 2021).

Sometimes even the possibility of a deepfake can have serious political ramifications. For example, when the President of Gabon, Ali Bongo, was hospitalised and disappeared from public life for a prolonged period of time, a newly-released video of him, instead of alleviating concern and putting to rest the rumours of his frail health or even death, only sparked rumours and conspiracy theories of it being a deepfake, ultimately providing an excuse for a coup attempt that only narrowly failed to succeed (McPeak, 2021, p. 440). While the authenticity of the abovementioned video remains inconclusive, at the time of writing (mid-2021), Ali Bongo is alive and in power. A further category of note would be journalists. Indeed, should a journalist be misled by a deepfake, there would be manifold damage, from the more immediate amplification of disinformation to broader matters, such as diminishing credibility of conventional media and erosion of trust in any information altogether—although sometimes all that is needed is for a journalist's account to be hacked to make the spread more convincing (Fischer, 2021). A seemingly more exotic, but no less potent, use has been the application of deepfake technology to manipulate satellite images; this could have multiple applications, from distorting maps to providing fake proof (Knight, 2021). One only has to think of, for example, the use of satellite imagery by the Bush administration to 'prove' the existence of weapons of mass destruction in Iraq or the images manufactured by Russia to frame Ukrainians for shooting down MH17 to realise that deepfake satellite imagery has potential for severe damage by making such attempts easier to carry out.

Crucially though, Simonite (2019) seems to be largely correct in asserting that the major threat of deepfakes, at least as of yet, is probably not impersonation of politicians, but 'amplifying local harassment' of activists and journalists instead of 'changing the fate of nations by felling national politicians'. However, implying a strong difference between these two levels and perceiving deepfake impersonations of non-high-profile individuals as a lesser threat, might be both deceptive and dangerous. In this regard, there already are documented cases of deepfakes being used to, for example, harass and undermine the reputations of journalists and activists (particularly female), critical of the government or other powerful actors, by disseminating deepfake pornography with their faces morphed into the videos (Greengard, 2020, p. 18; Maddalena & Gili, 2020, p. 16; Reid, 2021, p. 210). The potential is also present to not only verbally label such activists foreign agents, associates of criminal actors etc., which is already a popular strategy among non-democratic politicians (see e.g. Pomerantsev, 2019), but also to manufacture deepfake 'proof' of such connections.

In addition, deepfakes could significantly disrupt the litigation process—there already have been examples of falsified deepfake evidence appearing before court; that, again, poses the same two threats as for the society as a whole: the threat that a high-quality fake will remain undetected, potentially determining the outcome of a case and the threat that even evidence that has not been tampered with will lose its value (Reynolds, 2020; Breen, 2021, pp. 124–125; McPeak, 2021, p. 438). That also raises significant challenges for lawyers who now need to take extra care before submitting any evidence provided by their clients (Reynolds, 2020) and for the judicial process more broadly, particularly when it comes to admissibility and verification (Breen, 2021; McPeak, 2021). Likewise, exposing actual crimes, from bribery to crimes against humanity, is becoming more difficult because any evidence can simply be dismissed as deepfake (Pradhan, 2020; Gregory, 2021). In this way, the very nature of evidence and how it is provided before courts might have to be rethought (McPeak, 2021; see also European Parliamentary Research Service, 2021, p. 32).

Simultaneously, though, deepfake technology should not be reduced to its negative uses, becoming a new content category on its own right (Pesetski, 2020) and offering potential benefits in fields such as 'entertainment and education, from multilingual advertising campaigns [. . .] to bringing dead artists "back to life" to engage museum-goers' to audio-visually enriching school curricula (Diakopoulos & Johnson, 2020, p. 2). Educational benefits may also be considerable, such as 'resurrecting' people or reconstructing events (Fallis, 2020, pp. 4–5). In this sense, deepfakes hold the promise of 'resurrecting the past' and doing so in a way that appears to 'foster a sense of kinship' and provide emotional engagement in a way that would be impossible or very unlikely in case of traditional media (Mihailova, 2021); the Dalí Museum's deepfake resurrection of the surrealist painter is an oft-cited illustration of this point. Moreover, classes delivered by deepfake teachers and lecturers (potentially tailor-made to each student's needs and/or interests) would also be merely a further step in the direction of automation that is happening across industries and professions (Fallis, 2020, p. 5). What such attempts point towards could be identified as user experience personalisation and enhancement of marketing techniques, whereby such immersion serves as a tool for not only attention attraction but also the 'hooking' of target users or consumers (Kwok & Koh, 2021). Moreover, deepfakes can be used in advertising, film or any other audio-visual content to remove language barriers (Whittaker et al., 2020, p. 96). An example could be a video for the *Malaria Must Die* campaign in which the former footballer David Beckham is shown speaking nine different languages (Whittaker et al., 2021, p. 4). Another example might be that of Manoj Tiwari, an Indian politician, using deepfake technology to appear to be speaking different languages in a campaign video (see e.g. Jee, 2020).

More broadly, deepfakes open up opportunities for content creation unconstrained by language and the physical existence of those depicted (who could be living, dead, or fictional), all easily malleable in accordance with industry needs (Debusmann, 2021). Such a proposition appears to be particularly attractive in the film industry, where it could be used, among other things, for de-aging actors, such as for *The Irishman*, just much cheaper, as already demonstrated by a YouTube user using free software (Whittaker et al., 2020, p. 96). Another use is 'resurrecting' dead actors—even despite, unsurprisingly, involving 'an ethical and potentially legal minefield' (Whittaker et al., 2020, p. 96). The combination of the commercial allure of such (re)creations and the development of the necessary digital tools is driving the cinema industry to explore 'the aesthetic possibilities of such spectral, "ghostly" apparitions' (Holliday, 2021, p. 2).

Another promising avenue is the creation of artificial fashion models or brand ambassadors (Whittaker et al., 2020, p. 97), potentially tapping into the growing prominence of virtual influencers (see Kalpokas, 2021). Digital assistants can also be created in the image of the user to help them tackle everyday tasks online (Maddalena & Gili, 2020, p. 16), either as workload-reduction tools or in cases where the user would be otherwise physically or psychologically challenged. Meanwhile, in news broadcasting, deepfakes could be used to create virtual news anchors (which has already happened—see e.g. Debusmann, 2021) for either regular or breaking news broadcasts or, potentially, for personalised news programmes that would be algorithmically curated to an individual viewer's tastes, interests, and other preferences. Deepfakes can also be used for personalised media generation in the broad sense, such as inserting oneself into famous films (Whittaker et al., 2020, p. 97). Likewise, deepfakes offer new opportunities for consumer engagement, such as making it possible for individuals to become part of personalised advertising campaigns that can subsequently be shared on their social media accounts (Whittaker et al., 2020, p. 97; Whittaker et al., 2021, p. 4). With the above in mind, the claims of deepfakes being 'the future of content creation' (Debusmann, 2021) do not seem to be particularly outlandish or overblown.

Overall, then, deepfakes are best seen as a socio-technical phenomenon, underpinned by the use of the GAN technique and deep learning more broadly but simultaneously also co-constituted by the diverse drives behind its application in a social context. Hence, it is important to take into account the dense web of features and mutual influences that work simultaneously to co-constitute this increasingly complex form of synthetic media. Contrary to some of the overly simplistic accounts of deepfakes, the subsequent chapters will further contextualise them within the broader context of societal discourses, unexpected uses, and macro-level transformations.

References

Amer, P., Panetta, F., & Harrell, D. F. (2021, March). Combatting disinformation: Putting deepfakes in perspective. *Goethe Institut*, https://www.goethe.de/prj/k40/en/fil/dee.html
Andrejevic, M. (2020). *Automated media*. Routledge.
Bateman, J. (2020, August 10). Get ready for deepfakes to be used in financial scams. Carnegie Endowment for International Peace, https://carnegieendowment.org/2020/08/10/get-ready-for-deepfakes-to-be-used-in-financial-scams-pub-82469
Boden, M. A. (2018). *Artificial intelligence: A very short introduction*. Oxford University Press.

Bown, O. (2021). *Beyond the creative species: Making machines that make art and music.* The MIT Press.

Breen, D. C. (2021). Silent no more: How deepfakes will force courts to reconsider video admission standards. *Journal of High Technology Law, 21*(1), 122–161.

Burgess, M. (2020, October 21). A deepfake bot is being used to abuse thousands of women. *Wired*, https://www.wired.com/story/a-deepfake-porn-bot-is-being-used-to-abuse-thousands-of-women/

Chesney, R., & Citron, D. (2019). Deepfakes and the new disinformation war: The coming of age of post-truth geopolitics. *Foreign Affairs, 98*(1), 147–155.

Clahane, P. (2020, October 28). Fake naked photos of thousands of women shared online. *BBC*, https://www.bbc.com/news/technology-54584127

Debusmann, B. (2021, March 8). Deepfake is the Future of Content Creation. *BBC*, https://www.bbc.com/news/business-56278411

Diakopoulos, N., & Johnson, D. (2020). Anticipating and addressing the ethical implications of deepfakes in the context of elections. *New Media & Society.* https://doi.org/10.1177/1461444820925811

European Parliamentary Research Service. (2021). *Tackling Deepfakes in European Policy*, https://www.europarl.europa.eu/thinktank/en/document.html?reference=EPRS_STU(2021)690039

Fallis, D. (2020). The epistemic threat of deepfakes. *Philosophy and Technology.* https://doi.org/10.1007/s13347-020-00419-2

Fischer, S. (2021, February 2). Journalist identities hijacked to spread fake news. Axios, https://www.axios.com/journalist-identity-theft-hacks-fake-news-1a5bb3b0-fe8e-4bec-b0d4-beace3001aed.html

Galston, W. A. (2020, January 8). Is seeing still believing? The deepfake challenge to truth in politics. *Brookings*, https://www.brookings.edu/research/is-seeing-still-believing-the-deepfake-challenge-to-truth-in-politics/, Accessed 7 Feb 2020.

Giles, K., Hartmann, K., & Mustaffa, M. (2019). *The role of deepfakes in malign influence campaigns.* NATO StratCom COE.

Gosse, C., & Burkell, J. (2020). Politics and porn: How news media characterizes problems presented by deepfakes. *Critical Studies in Media Communication, 37*(5), 497–511.

Gow, G. (2021, May 2). The scary truth behind the FBI warning: Deepfake fraud is here and it's serious—We are not prepared. *Forbes*, https://www.forbes.com/sites/glenngow/2021/05/02/the-scary-truth-behind-the-fbi-warning-deepfake-fraud-is-here-and-its-serious-we-are-not-prepared/?sh=9a5c39531799

Greengard, S. (2019). *Virtual reality.* The MIT Press.

Greengard, S. (2020). Will deepfakes do deep damage? *Society, 63*(1), 17–19.

Gregory, S. (2021, February 14). Authoritarian regimes could exploit cries of 'Deepfake', *Wired*, https://www.wired.com/story/opinion-authoritarian-regimes-could-exploit-cries-of-deepfake/

Holliday, C. (2021). Rewriting the stars: Surface tensions and gender troubles in the online media production of digital deepfakes. *Convergence: The International Journal of Research into New Media Technologies.* https://doi.org/10.1177/13548565211029412

Jee, C. (2020, February 19). An Indian Politician is using deepfake technology to win new voters. *MIT Technology Review*, https://www.technologyreview.com/2020/02/19/868173/an-indian-politician-is-using-deepfakes-to-try-and-win-voters/

Kalpokas, I. (2021). Problematising reality: The promises and perils of synthetic media. *SN Social Sciences, 1*(1), 1–11.

Kaplan, M. (2019). The digital potlatch: The uses of uselessness in the digital economy. *New Media & Society, 21*(9), 1947–1966.

Kelleher, J. D. (2019). *Deep learning.* The MIT Press.

Kikerpill, K. (2020). Choose your stars and studs: The rise of deepfake designer porn. *Porn Studies, 7*(4), 352–356.

Kirchengast, T. (2020). Deepfakes and image manipulation: Criminalisation and control. *Information and Telecommunications Technology Law, 29*(3), 308–323.

Knight, W. (2021, May 28). Deepfake maps could really mess with your sense of the World. *Wired*, https://www.wired.com/story/deepfake-maps-mess-sense-world/

Kwok, A. O. J., & Koh, S. G. M. (2021). Deepfake: A social construction of technology perspective. *Current Issues in Tourism, 24*(13), 1798–1802.

Lee, D. (2018, February 3). Deepfakes porn has serious consequences. *BBC*, https://www.bbc.com/news/technology-42912529

Maddalena, G., & Gili, G. (2020). *The history and theory of post-truth communication*. Palgrave Macmillan.

Maddocks, S. (2020). 'A Deepfake Plot Intended to Silence Me': Exploring continuities between pornographic and 'Political' deep fakes. *Porn Studies, 7*(4), 415–423.

Martineu, P. (2019, December 20). Facebook removes accounts with ai-generated profile photos. *Wired*, Available at: https://www.wired.com/story/facebook-removes-accounts-ai-generated-photos/

McPeak, A. (2021). The threat of deepfakes in litigation: Raising the authentication bar to combat falsehood. *Vanderbilt Journal of Entertainment and Technology Law, 23*(2), 433–450.

Mihailova, M. (2021). To dally with Dalí: Deepfake (Inter)faces in the art museum. *Convergence: The International Journal of Research into New Media Technologies*. https://doi.org/10.1177/13548565211029401

Noone, G. (2021, February 4). Listen carefully: The growing threat of audio deepfake scams. *TechMonitor*, https://techmonitor.ai/techonology/cybersecurity/growing-threat-audio-deepfake-scams

Pesetski, A. (2020). Deepfakes: A new content category for a digital age. *William & Mary Bill of Rights Journal, 29*(2), 503–532.

Pomerantsev, P. (2019). *This is not propaganda: Adventures in the war against reality*. Faber & Faber.

Popova, M. (2020). Reading out of context: Pornographic deepfakes, celebrity and intimacy. *Porn Studies, 7*(4), 367–381.

Pradhan, P. (2020, October 4). AI Deepfakes: The goose is cooked? *University of Illinois Law Review*, https://www.illinoislawreview.org/blog/ai-deepfakes/

Rafaghello, I., Kastalio, L., Kalf, S., & Paisley, E. (2019, October 24). What does a feminist approach to deepfake pornography look like? *Masters of Media*, http://mastersofmedia.hum.uva.nl/blog/2019/10/24/what-does-a-feminist-approach-to-deepfake-pornography-look-like/

Reid, S. (2021). The deepfake dilemma: Reconciling privacy and first amendment protections. *University of Pennsylvania Journal of Constitutional Law, 23*(1), 209–237.

Reynolds, M. (2020, June 9). Courts and lawyers struggle with growing prevalence of deepfakes. *American Bar Association Journal*, https://www.abajournal.com/web/article/courts-and-lawyers-struggle-with-growing-prevalence-of-deepfakes

Selbie, T., & Williams, C. (2021, May 27). Deepfake pornography could become epidemic, expert warns, *BBC*, https://www.bbc.com/news/uk-scotland-57254636

Shane, J. (2020). *You look like a thing and I Love You*. Wildfire.

Siggelkow, N., & Terwiesch, C. (2019). *Connected strategy: Building continuous customer relationships for competitive advantage*. Harvard Business Review Press.

Simonite, T. (2019, September 4). Forget politics: For now, deepfakes are for bullies. *Wired*, https://www.wired.com/story/forget-politics-deepfakes-bullies/

Simonite, T. (2020, May 8). Cheap, easy deepfakes are getting closer to the real thing. *Wired*, https://www.wired.com/story/cheap-easy-deepfakes-closer-real-thing/

Statt, N. (2018, January 24). Fake celebrity porn is blowing up on reddit, thanks to artificial intelligence. *The Verge*, https://www.theverge.com/2018/1/24/16929148/fake-celebrity-porn-ai-deepfake-face-swapping-artificial-intelligence-reddit

The Baltic Times. (2021, April 22). Person pretending to be Navalny's rep carried out provocative attacks against baltics, https://www.baltictimes.com/person_pretending_to_be_navalny_s_rep_carried_out_provocative_attacks_against_baltics/

Whittaker, L., et al. (2020). 'All around me are synthetic faces': The mad world of AI-generated media. *IT Professional, 22*(5), 90–99.

Whittaker, L., Letheren, K., & Mulcahy, R. (2021). The rise of deepfakes: A conceptual framework and research agenda for marketing. *Australasian Marketing Journal.* https://doi.org/10.1177/1839334921999479

Wilkerson, L. (2021). Still waters run deep(fakes): The rising concerns of 'Deepfake' technology and its influence on democracy and the first amendment. *Missouri Law Review, 86*(1), 407–432.

Woolley, S. (2020). *The reality game: How the next wave of technology will break the truth and what we can do about it.* Endeavour.

Woolley, S., & Joseff, K. (2020). *Demand for deceit: How the way we think drives disinformation.* National Endowment for Democracy and International Forum for Democratic Studies, available at: https://www.ned.org/wp-content/uploads/2020/01/Demand-for-Deceit.pdf

Young, N. (2019). *Deepfake technology: Complete guide to deepfakes, politics and social media.* Independently published

Chapter 5
On Alarmism: Between Infodemic and Epistemic Anarchy

Authors currently writing on deepfakes frequently do not shy away from strong and impactful assessments. It has become commonplace to assert, as, for example, Whittaker et al. (2020, p. 95) do, that '[d]eepfakes and GANs represent the next generation of fake news and threaten to further erode trust in online information' due to the difficulty in spotting the manipulation, particularly when one takes cognitive biases and the structural features of today's media, such as echo chambers, into account. Hence, as Breen (2021, p. 123) argues, deepfakes 'take disinformation to the next level' by 'further complicat[ing] the ability to decipher true information'. Similarly, Whittaker et al. (2021, p. 5) emphasise a combination of low barrier of entry (as deepfakes can be easily created even by those with limited skills and resources), the ease of sharing content on social media, and the ever-growing amount of digital material featuring a vast proportion of the global population that can be used as training data as a major point of concern. Seen in this light, deepfakes 'can have a massive impact on public perception of events' (Breen 2021, p. 145). Hence, the popular narrative goes, 'artificially generated content will further fuel the fake news crisis with their ability to undermine truth and confuse viewers' (Whittaker et al., 2020, p. 95). The identified negative effects are fundamental, such as 'distortion of democratic discourse, eroding trust in institutions and journalism, increasing social divisions, and threats to national security' (Wilkerson, 2021, p. 412). The stakes seemingly cannot be higher—after all, as Huston and Bahm (2020) warn, '[t]ruth is under attack' in what Schick (2020) describes as the 'Infocalypse', a world allegedly oversaturated with disinformation and manipulation to the extent that the public sphere is effectively destroyed, with deepfakes seen as a major contributing factor. Nevertheless, as will be shown in this chapter and subsequently in this book, such accounts give simultaneously too much and too little credit to deepfakes.

Johnson and Diakopoulos (2021, p. 33) usefully distinguish between three different kinds of deepfake harm: they 'can harm *viewers* by deceiving or intimidating, harm *subjects* by causing reputational damage, and harm *society* by undermining societal values such as trust in institutions'. Indeed, the worry is that due to the increasing proliferation and advancement of deepfakes, portraying events

© The Author(s), under exclusive license to Springer Nature Switzerland AG 2022
I. Kalpokas, J. Kalpokiene, *Deepfakes*, SpringerBriefs in Political Science,
https://doi.org/10.1007/978-3-030-93802-4_5

or actions that never took place is becoming increasingly unproblematic (Chesney & Citron, 2019, p. 148). Hence, '[d]eepfakes could be used to challenge public opinion and what we know as reality in basically all sectors of culture and society' (Woolley, 2020, p. 107). Even more extensively, for Woolley and Joseff (2020, p. 23), '[i]n the political domain, manipulated and synthesized audio and visual content might be used to affect diplomatic negotiations, incite conflicts, and manipulate elections' while, no less importantly, '[i]n the social domain, they could be employed to exacerbate polarization and demographic divisions or erode trust in institutions, among other outcomes'. Hence, societal and political order can be seriously undermined, particularly keeping in mind the prevalence of and susceptibility to fake content of all kinds, discussed earlier in this book.

When considering why deepfakes are seen as a particularly potent addition to the disinformation arsenal, it is crucial to keep in mind that visual imagery obtains considerable importance in today's context of information overabundance and content excess: it is particularly suitable for fast-paced consumption, particularly because it is 'immediate, easy-to-digest, and elicits emotion' (Seo, 2020, p. 129). Similarly, McPeak (2021, p. 439) stresses that '[m]any people value visual perception above other indicators of truth'—a development that has been only strengthened by the rise of social media and, particularly, image- and video-centric platforms, such as Instagram, YouTube, and TikTok. While the primacy of video is clearly a broader feature of contemporary digital culture, the key source of concern about deepfakes relates to the long-accepted truism that seeing is believing, implying that visual media typically are accepted at face value as reliable proof to support words— and with deepfakes, it seems, that can no longer hold (Maras & Alexandrou, 2019, p. 257; see also Ahmed, 2021, p. 2; Whittaker et al., 2021, p. 5).

In light of the above, deepfakes are likely to usher in an era in which such old certainties no longer hold, tapping into the broader transformation of disinformation strategies, whereby instead of promotion of a single propaganda narrative, the new kind of disinformation 'divides and deceives populations' (Jankowicz, 2020, p. xvii; see also Bastos et al., 2021, p. 15). Indeed, while a pure lie, which can be universally dismissed by all audiences is 'flat' and often ineffective, a more complex web of targeted fakery, obfuscation, and manipulation is much more likely to do the job by more immediately sticking to the most receptive part of the population, pitting them against other parts of the society that have been matched with a competing, albeit likely equally manipulated, message (Maddalena & Gili, 2020, pp. 29–30). It is here that sheer quantity of messages, targeted to different tastes and information literacy skills, is necessary, highlighting the importance of generation technology—as Huston and Bahm (2020) pinpoint, [w]hile the harmful use of (mis)information has been around for centuries, technology now allows this to happen at a speed and scale never before seen'. Hence, just like the advent of AI is typically associated with automation and greater efficiency across different settings, so is likely to happen in disinformation as well.

This situation leaves societies with few good options: on the one hand, in order to minimise the effects of deepfake manipulation, everything must be treated with suspicion (Joseph, 2019; see also Diakopoulos & Johnson, 2020, p. 3) while on the other hand, such suspicion would only lead to a paranoid and incapacitated public sphere, which might in itself be what the threat actors had wanted. After all, such paranoia would have 'serious ramifications for politics, but also for trust and security in business, civil society, the arts, and – more generally – everyday life' (Woolley, 2020, p. 107). That, in turn, would likely lead to the preponderance of 'acquiescence, not belief' when 'everything, and nothing, is believable anymore', thereby causing political paralysis through division and confusion (O'Shaughnessy, 2020, pp. 58–59). In this way, 'shared beliefs among the citizenry can be undermined if the populations ceased to believe they are part of a common community that encourages reciprocal trust' (Bastos et al., 2021, p. 15). Clearly, under such circumstances, deepfakes and other AI-generated content 'may lead to a world in which it is no longer clear what is true and what is false, where facts and fiction mix' (Coeckelbergh, 2020, p. 103). Similarly, Amer et al. (2021) warn of a 'zero-trust' society, in which everything and anything could equally plausibly be true, fake, or in-between. And there already is research to suggest that even under current levels of technological sophistication, such erosion of trust is a very likely outcome, leading to apathy and cynicism (see Vaccari & Chadwick, 2020; Reid, 2021, p. 211).

Crucially, as Whittaker et al. (2021, p. 5) emphasise, 'deepfakes do not need to deceive to do damage'—it is sufficient for deception potential to exist to sow confusion and undermine civic life. In fact, some early research suggests that not just exposure to but even awareness of and concern about deepfakes are sufficient to reduce trust in online informational content, particularly on social media (Ahmed, 2021, p. 15). Hence, here we return to another issue stressed previously in the book: if nothing can be proven absolutely, but everything is easily available online, then why not opt for content that at least fits one's worldview unproblematically. Deepfakes here could be seen as enabling a two-pronged attack: on the one hand, sowing confusion and thereby lowering the bar for alternative narratives and truth-candidates while, on the other hand, making one or more of such challenger narratives more plausible by adding visual support that could pass as a good enough proof or, at the very least, illustration—again, it must be remembered that visualisations of any sorts add extra credibility to a story.

Under conditions of such 'epistemological anarchy', it will simply be easier for voters to 'remain within their partisan bubbles, believing only those politicians and media figures who share their political orientation' (Galston, 2020). To that effect, the true target (and, potentially, victim) or deepfakes could be not (solely) those impersonated but, even more importantly, any shared sense of authenticity and proof (Maddalena & Gili, 2020, p. 16). Hence, in this polarised environment '[n]either side can persuade or convince the other' as 'each attempt only risks entrenching further division' (Schick, 2020, p. 12). While deepfakes cannot be credited as either the cause or even as the most important driving factor (the underlying datafication and algorithmisation processes remain paramount—see e.g. Kalpokas, 2021a), they are, nevertheless, an important tool by which these processes take place. At the very least, deepfakes are increasing complexity and making the gathering and convincing presentation of evidence more difficult, making even factual information significantly less believable (Koenig, 2019; Whittaker et al., 2021, p. 5). No less importantly, this situation also offers the opportunity for politicians and other individuals who actually *are* involved in potentially embarrassing or even illegal affairs to cast doubt on any evidence by simply using 'the rise of these altered videos to claim that they were framed' (Woolley, 2020, p. 14; see also Fallis, 2020; Galston, 2020, Vaccari & Chadwick, 2020; Whittaker et al., 2020, p. 95), thereby leading to further delegitimization of facts (Ahmed, 2021, p. 2). Under such conditions, arriving at substantive agreement of any sort and, therefore, setting a course of action, the legitimacy (if not the content) of which is believed in by the majority of relevant actors, might become impossible. After all, the threat actors often do not need their targets to adopt a new mindset or change their core beliefs—it often suffices that people abstain from siding with a cause, turning up to vote etc. (Hendricks & Vestergaard, 2019, p. 15).

Under conditions described above, it is tempting to agree with the concern that deepfakes have the potential to undermine democracy (see e.g. Reid, 2021, p. 211), particularly by contributing to what RAND researchers have recently called 'truth decay' (see Mazarr et al., 2019). And that is precisely the point—the issue is not about replacement of *the* Truth with some fake imitation of it, not necessarily about imprinting a propaganda master narrative into the minds of audiences—after all, some early experimental evidence suggests that deepfakes may not be much more effective than well-constructed textual narratives in instilling false memories (see Murphy & Flynn, 2021)—but about creating an ever-moving kaleidoscope of truth-candidates that ultimately undermine any possibility for a meaningful public sphere. Here, one must consider the importance of one's lifeworld, which entails 'the impressions, activities and relationships that make up the world as a person experiences it and people in shared contexts experience it together' while, in their digital form, such lifeworlds increasingly 'connect humans, sophisticated machines and abundant data' (Kerner & Risse, 2021, p. 82; see also Susskind, 2018). Manipulating such lifeworld has the effect of essentially hacking the experience of and, consequently, decision-making rules for the everyday at an individual and/or group level. Again, it must be stressed that the lifeworld, in which we subjectively dwell, is about experience of, and not direct access to, the everyday—and this is what makes it malleable and vulnerable. Seen in this light, 'truth decay' is the decay of points in common between different individual- or group-level lifeworlds. Hence, we should worry less about isolated high-impact deepfakes but about the cumulative impact of routinised use of low- and medium-profile ones.

Importantly, a further threat can be seen in the sense of entitlement to have one's fantasies fulfilled. That entitlement is clearly evident already in the very existence of so-called 'undressing apps' and deepfake pornography more broadly as well as in the drive towards personalisation (including through the use of deepfakes), sketched out previously in this book. While such sense of entitlement might lead to designer information environments (whereby individuals either actively structure the news content consumed or have it structured through, often algorithmic, curation—see e.g. Kalpokas, 2018), it is certainly evident in the drive towards 'designer pornography'. As Kikerpill (2020, p. 353) writes, [c]hoosing a fantasy to be played out is one thing, but choosing the players from a pool that includes everyone in the world, barring those without any real online presence, is on a different level altogether', particularly when one considers online forums not just catering for any deepfake fantasy but also offering custom-made pornographic deepfakes, e.g. of one's sweetheart from years ago. In fact, not just the output, but the backend story tends to be demeaning—as Bode (2021, p. 14) observes, in online forums dedicated to deepfake creation, the human dimension tends to be abstracted away as participants 'discuss faces as data objects to be played with rather than as properties of a person'. In this way, any concern about anything beyond the self is lost, with objectification and exploitation for personal satisfaction taking hold (see e.g. Newton and Stanfill 2020; Popova 2020). As it is often the case with the developments discussed in this book, such trends are often difficul to separate: for example, very selective information consumption and highly objectifying fantasies about women closely coexist in Alt-Right communities (see e.g. Nagle, 2017). Even more broadly, though, this me-centricity is likely to extend ever deeper towards the core of the societal fabric, building on the drive for ordering and domination that is historically premised on toxic white masculinity (see, notably, Grear, 2015) but by now potentially expandable even beyond the white male core as a me-centric drive for dominating the world.

Indeed, pervasive (to the extent of turning toxic) me-centricity should be seen as located at the heart of today's user experience, resulting in spoiled audiences that expect everything to bring satisfaction. With audience- and consumer-centricity being all the rage in today's business world, consumer experience is datafied, segmented, and re-aggregated to be more conveniently manageable for the provider and more pleasurable for the end-user in an economy where everything happens 'now' and must be immediately relevant (see e.g. Weinstein, 2020; Hodkinson et al., 2021), building on deep and intimate knowledge of every target individual (Yu, 2021). Entire business practices—and businesses themselves—allegedly need to be overhauled to best serve their end-user base by not just employing but also building upon big data and analytics (see, characteristically, Morgan, 2021; Shah & Murthi, 2021; Wild, 2021). Deep learning and other advanced technologies here often take centre stage as well, almost as a kind of magic bullet (see e.g. Rizzo et al., 2020). Such trends, however, are by no means limited to business but extend, as mentioned above, to the provision of news and other kinds of information as well as to political leadership practices that prioritise audience satisfaction above everything else (see Kalpokas, 2019, 2021b). Hence, deepfakes should not be seen as simply a tool for deception, abuse, perverse self-gratification, or simply personalised non-nefarious content creation: they are a further step it the direction of me-centricity (and expectation, even a feeling of entitlement to it).

Another point of concern is the relatively democratic nature of deepfakes as political disruption no longer necessitates significant skill or cutting-edge technology. As Fallis (2020, p. 4) puts it, '[m]achine learning can make it possible for *almost anyone* to create convincing fake videos of *anyone* doing or saying *anything*'. Similarly, for Huston and Bahm (2020), [w]ith the proliferation of technology, a teenager sitting at home can create and distribute a high-quality deepfake video on her smartphone in a single afternoon'. This description is eerily similar to the old stereotypical image of a teenage hacker, promoted by films like *War Games*

(1983)—until the cyber threat landscape became a much more grown-up affair that it is today. Nevertheless, despite the stereotyping, the crucial point about accessibility still holds. Indeed, 'deepfakes give both individuals and organizations the power to create highly realistic, yet synthetic representations of whoever they please' (Whittaker et al., 2021, p. 3). Unlike, for example, photo editing software, which typically requires a high level of skill to produce realistically-looking doctored images, GANs only require input material from which content will be generated and a sufficiently powerful computer (although the necessary infrastructure can equally be rented as a service via the cloud) while the fakery is produced by the algorithms themselves (Young, 2019, p. 13). Moreover, the accessibility of deepfake making is further increased by much of the software being freely and openly available online. At the moment, the only major limiting factor is the amount of input content necessary for creating a high-fidelity deepfake, although that is bound to decrease as well. In fact, there is already software for creating lower-fidelity fakes from merely a set of photos taken from all sides while it is also possible to produce low-quality fakes from a single image (see e.g. Solsman, 2019; Hearn, 2021). Moreover, even in case of the more input-intensive techniques, it must be admitted, as a result of social media and other kinds of online presence, 'there are sufficiently large amounts of audio, video, picture, and text materials online, provided voluntarily or otherwise' to put most people at some risk of impersonation (Giles et al., 2019, p. 17), leading Schick (2020, p. 145) to declare that 'everyone is at risk'. In addition to non-consensual deepfake pornography, the use of the technology for private intimidation, score-settling, or even the most trivial matters, as in the case of a mother creating deepfakes to frame her daughter's competitors in a cheerleading competition (see e.g. Brown, 2021), only further underscore such an assertion.

Since rapid dissemination, consumption, and reproduction of digital content are now the norm, the detrimental effects suffered by the victims (politicians falsely implicated in malicious activities, populations nudged towards societally suboptimal choices etc.) will likely be long-lasting. Even despite some platforms (Facebook, perhaps, most prominently) banning deepfake content, it is only removed after being identified and reported (hence, if it is placed in a sympathetic environment, reporting might not even occur); and even if such content is removed or in case automatic content filtering is applied, it can easily reappear on a different platform, forum, or group frequented by the Maras & Alexandrou, 2019, p. 257). Also, as with fact-checking or any digital forensics, deepfake detection is not only reactive in its nature but is also typically more time-consuming than the generation of fake content itself; as a result, deepfakes will probably remain undisproved (and reach large numbers of people) before their artificial nature can be demonstrated convincingly (Galston, 2020). Ultimately, while detection is always a race against time (to disprove fake content as soon as possible) and technology (to overcome the latest innovations in deepfake technology), 'the forgers might only need to place one video in the right place at the right time to achieve their goal' (Thomas, 2019). And, as to the last point, there is no guarantee that by that time target audiences, having invested time, reputation, and other resources in the alleged veracity of the fake, would be willing to change their mind on the matter. The latter point is not merely hypothetical: as shown by the uptake and sustained effect of fake news and other kinds of deception, lack of veracity is by no means an obstacle to influence—on the contrary, it can become an asset through catering to audience wants, needs, and desires. But once video content is added to the equation, the believability of fake content increases even further (Hall, 2018, p. 52).

Furthermore, persistent deepfake attacks against journalists and activists, from NGO representatives to celebrities taking up public causes (see Maddocks, 2020), would probably be even more corrosive of democracy than isolated ones against seasoned politicians. The reason is that the looming and persistent threat of being deepfaked and having one's reputation destroyed would likely create an atmosphere of fear, whereby very few would be willing to step up and question or challenge the methods and policies of those in power. Moreover, deepfakes targeting journalists and activists also are less likely to be debunked: first, they will probably receive less scrutiny than ones featuring high-flying politicians; second, journalists and activists typically have less public schedules, so they are less likely to have proof of verifiably having been elsewhere (e.g. at a public event) when the alleged misdemeanour supposedly occurred; third, journalists and activists (excluding celebrities) are likely to have less access to legal, forensic, and image repair teams that could help withstand the effect and limit the spread of deepfakes.

Nevertheless, the above is not to imply that high-profile politicians are somehow immune from being substantially harmed. The key factor here might well be the timing of the attack: for example, if a an unfavourable deepfake video appears on the eve of a tightly contested election, there may no longer be enough time to respond properly, but sufficient numbers of people could be tricked into voting for the opponent, or at least put into doubt, dissuading them from casting their vote at all (Charlet & Citron, 2019). Also, even at a longer time distance and in the presence of a well-orchestrated response, as long as the deepfake ends up in a fertile (or at least susceptible) soil, neither debunking nor the likely absence of full realism (at least as far as the present technology is concerned) may be sufficient to dissuade people from believing the fake. Still, it must be stressed that despite the alarmist accounts of deepfakes spilling much ink on precisely this typo of use, it is, at least for the time being, unlikely to go mainstream due to the difficulty of successfully pulling of this kind of attack and unavoidable post-hoc scrutiny that is likely to lead to a backlash against the perpetrator. Lower, profile deepfakes, meanwhile, even if routinely used, are significantly less likely to cross the threshold of significant action being taken. Crucially, the latter are also likely to be more immune to potential regulation (discussed in greater detail later in this book).

Certainly, the deepfakes that we have seen to date (at least at the time of writing) can, with greater or lesser effort, be detected as such, even with a naked eye, although with the advancement of technology that might become ever more difficult (Breen, 2021, p. 124; Whittaker et al., 2021, p. 3), prompting a search for new technological solutions. For example, Facebook has recently touted its new deepfake-detection tool (developed with Michigan State University) to reverse-engineer AI-generated images (Yin & Hassner, 2021). However, such detectability might not necessarily matter—at least not immediately. As stressed previously in the book, users often embrace content not because of its truthlikeness or as a result of extended factchecking of the claims made. Instead, the content that offers clear cognitive benefits by fitting nicely into pre-existing schemes, confirming already held biases, and being generally easily accessible and consumable is, under typical circumstances, much more likely to get accepted than the competing truth-claims.

Indeed, as meaning and gratification, and not the detail, constitute the value of content in this environment where audiences are spoilt for choice, a deepfake of acceptable quality is likely to gain traction, and once it does, its virality metrics will do the rest of the work to push it upwards in the visibility pecking order. Moreover, what passes as 'acceptable quality' is also up for debate. After all, as we are all by now used to often grainy and glitchy Zoom videos, the bar might not even be particularly high (Golingai, 2019; Venkataramakrishnan, 2019; Tucker, 2020). Also, should such deepfakes land in an echo chamber susceptible to that precise manipulation (i.e. composed of people who chare a dislike for a politician who is unfavourably portrayed in that deepfake video), users may be driven to believe strongly enough to suspend critical thinking. For that reason, the presence of detection tools, instead of helping, might only lead to complacency and false sense of security. Moreover, as models are set to be improving by design, ever-more elaborate fake content is bound to be generated (Paul & Posard, 2020), thereby implying a constant arms race between generation and detection tools.

Still, much of the current debate about deepfakes is ignited more by panic than by fact and reasonable prediction. Already back in 2019, it was expected that '[s]oon (meaning months, not years), it may be impossible to tell real videos from fake ones' (Charlet & Citron, 2019), deceiving voters and swinging elections (Patersman & Hanley, 2020)—a prediction that, if taken verbatim, has by now turned out to be alarmist, confirming the dismissive arguments of some that concern about deepfakes is driven more by 'dramatic anecdotes' rather than hard facts, of which there are only a few anyway (see e.g. Simonite, 2019). Likewise, there seems to be a sense of time desperately running out, of impending doom (see e.g. Schick, 2020, pp. 190–192)— after all, what else terms such as the 'Infocalypse' could denote. However, while the full realisation of deepfake potential might, after all, take years, not months, as already stressed, often there is no need for completely reality-like content, particularly if the video ends up in fertile soil. In addition, it must be stressed that 'the greatest lesson of the past few years lies not in the tactics employed by online propagandists, but the speed with which they change' (Woolley, 2020, p. 39), and deepfakes just naturally continue the trend both in their adoption and in the rapid pace of their development, meaning that they will ultimately find an important place in the disinformation arsenals of hostile state and non-state actors. Moreover, deepfakes also tap into the increasing shift towards interactive propaganda by offering easily consumable and easily shareable content that anyone can spread through their networks without putting much thought into it, thus becoming the manipulator's accomplice. And even if the content is debunked at some point, the difficulty in admitting an error of judgement (not only to others but also to oneself) might be a sufficient hurdle to prevent the users involved from backing down. After all, it is always 'not me' but, instead, the others who are seen as disseminating fakeries (Maddalena & Gili, 2020, p. 91; see also Lyons et al., 2021, p. 13).

According to the mainstream representations of threats, the transformation transpired to be both in kind and in scale. For example, according to Coeckelbergh (2020, p. 103), 'Film, for example, has always created illusions, and newspapers have spread propaganda. But with AI, combined with the possibilities and environment of the internet and digital social media, the problem seems to increase in intensity', leading to the conclusion that '[t]here seem to be more opportunities for manipulation, putting critical thinking at risk'. Similarly, to Wojewidka (2020), 'deepfakes are much closer to our perception of reality. They erase the line between reality and fantasy, genuine and fake, to the extent that the fundamental human ability to process the physical world is being more seriously challenged'. Again, this implies that routinisation and normalisation of deepfakes is going to be more impactful and more transformative than the typically expected singular election-transforming or war-triggering occurrences.

Simultaneously, progress and normalisation of deepfakes as a content generation technique 'is driven more by business realities than by adversaries waging information warfare'—certainly, virtual influencers and even virtual news anchors are not unheard of (Giles et al., 2019, p. 11). Moreover, as noted in the previous chapter, deep personalisation is likely to be the next big thing in digital consumer-oriented products more broadly, a continuation of the current drive to put as much personal touch into service as possible, and at least some social media platforms are creating in-built deepfake capacity to be opened up to the general user base (Constine, 2020). Nevertheless, such normalisation itself can easily become a source of concern, particularly if these are turned towards malicious ends and once techniques originally developed for marketing purposes become redirected towards political manipulation. In other words, if people are willing to follow virtual influencers while being fully aware of their virtuality and treat them with similar regard as they do human ones (see e.g. Kalpokas, 2021c), then the deception burden is removed as even openly virtual influencers can be used to promote political messages as they do commercial ones. The net result here becomes roughly comparable to that of deep astroturfing: simulation of opinion and influence, with a view to orchestrate audience ideas and behaviours. Likewise, while it can be partly agreed that 'deepfakes are most often (but not always) created, indexed, and received as a trick for the eye rather than with the intent to deceive in mind' (Bode, 2021, p. 13), this hardly makes them less nasty (for example, a noticeably glitchy deepfake porn video created for fun could be no less distressing—and, arguably, even more demeaning—for the victim).

Under such circumstances, it might be tempting to echo the sentiment of e.g. Hendricks and Vestergaard (2019) that reality has been somehow 'lost' without even pausing to think carefully whether it actually is—or whether direct access to it has ever been properly had. Particularly under conditions of deep mediatisation (see e.g. Hepp, 2020), it becomes difficult, if at all possible, to consider the experience of and acting in 'reality' as separate from its representation and even constitution by media of the most varied sorts. In this environment, as people become increasingly accustomed to and expectant of digital reality construction, high-profile deepfakes with whole-society impact may even become impossible as audiences simply refuse to take anything for granted. On the contrary, it is plausible deniability, or 'liar's dividend', as a side-effect, that is much more plausible. This, alongside cognitive disorientation (or epistemic anarchy) through a kaleidoscope of divergent and contradictory content, deepfake and otherwise, as well as further expansion of harassment, should be seen as the main takeaways on the likely effects of deepfakes.

The final question, then, remains as to why the focus on less plausible, yet dramatic, outcomes is so prevalent. A likely reason is that the debate on deepfakes, even in academic fora, is still highly dependent on journalistic discourse. As Wahl-Jorgensen and Carlson (2021) suggest, since deepfakes have entered public debate at a time of intense digital transformations and an ensuing weakening of journalistic authority and while debates around 'fake news' (again often blamed on journalism's demise) are still raging, this new technology has become a scapegoat and an amalgamation of everything that is bad in today's media environment. Moreover, such framing allows for a renewed lease of life to professional journalism—fighting disinformation in all the new and emergent forms—meaning that there might me be more than a hint of vested interest in the vilification of deepfakes (Wahl-Jorgensen & Carlson, 2021), particularly with the addition of headline-grabbing drama focused on predicted singular dramatic events.

References

Ahmed, S. (2021). Navigating the maze: Deepfakes, cognitive ability, and social media news scepticism. *New Media & Society*. https://doi.org/10.1177/14614448211019198

Amer, P., Panetta, F., & Harrell, D. F. (2021, March). Combatting disinformation: Putting deepfakes in perspective. *Goethe Institut*, https://www.goethe.de/prj/k40/en/fil/dee.html

Bastos, M., Mercea, D., & Goveia, F. (2021). Guy next door and implausibly attractive young women: The visual frames of social media propaganda. *New Media & Society*. https://doi.org/10.1177/14614448211026580

Bode, L. (2021). Deepfaking Keanu: YouTube deepfakes, platform visual effects, and the complexity of reception. *Convergence: International Journal of Research into New Media Technologies*. https://doi.org/10.1177/13548565211030454

Breen, D. C. (2021). Silent no more: How deepfakes will force courts to reconsider video admission standards. *Journal of High Technology Law, 21*(1), 122–161.

Brown, P. (2021, March 22). Three cheerleaders victimized by deepfake videos. *New York Law Journal*, https://www.law.com/newyorklawjournal/2021/03/22/three-cheerleaders-victimized-by-deepfake-videos/?slreturn=20210813074941

Charlet, K., & Citron, D. (2019, September 5). Campaigns must prepare for deepfakes: This is what their plan should look like. *Carnegie Endowment for International Peace*, https://carnegieendowment.org/2019/09/05/campaigns-must-prepare-for-deepfakes-this-is-what-their-plan-should-look-like-pub-79792

Chesney, R., & Citron, D. (2019). Deepfakes and the new disinformation war: The coming of age of post-truth geopolitics. *Foreign Affairs, 98*(1), 147–155.

Coeckelbergh, M. (2020). *AI Ethics*. The MIT Press.

Constine, J. (2020, January 3). ByteDance and TikTok have secretly built a deepfakes maker. *TechCrunch*, https://techcrunch.com/2020/01/03/tiktok-deepfakes-face-swap/

Diakopoulos, N., & Johnson, D. (2020). Anticipating and addressing the ethical implications of deepfakes in the context of elections. *New Media & Society.* https://doi.org/10.1177/1461444820925811

Fallis, D. (2020). The epistemic threat of deepfakes. *Philosophy and Technology.* https://doi.org/10.1007/s13347-020-00419-2

Galston, W. A. (2020, January 8). Is seeing still believing? The deepfake challenge to truth in politics. *Brookings Institution,* https://www.brookings.edu/research/is-seeing-still-believing-the-deepfake-challenge-to-truth-in-politics/

Giles, K., Hartmann, K., & Mustaffa, M. (2019). *The role of deepfakes in malign influence campaigns.* NATO StratCom COE.

Golingai, P. (2019, June 15). Is it Amin or a Deepfake?, *The Star,* https://www.thestar.com.my/opinion/columnists/one-mans-meat/2019/06/15/is-it-azmin-or-a-deepfake

Grear, A. (2015). Deconstructing *Anthropos*: A critical legal reflection on 'Anthropocentric' law and anthropocene 'Humanity'. *Law Critique, 26,* 225–249.

Hall, K. H. (2018). Deepfake videos: When seeing isn't believing. *Catholic University Journal of Law and Technology, 27*(1), 51–76.

Hearn, A. (2021, March 1). Deep nostalgia: 'Creepy' new service uses AI to animate old family photos. *The Guardian,* https://www.theguardian.com/technology/2021/mar/01/deep-nostalgia-creepy-new-service-ai-animate-old-family-photos

Hendricks, V. F., & Vestergaard, M. (2019). *Reality lost: Markets of attention, misinformation and manipulation.* Springer.

Hepp, A. (2020). *Deep mediatization.* Routledge.

Hodkinson, I. R., Jackson, T. W., & West, A. A. (2021). Customer experience management: Asking the right questions. *Journal of Business Strategy.* https://doi.org/10.1108/JBS-07-2020-0158

Huston, R. P., & Bahm, M. E. (2020). Deepfakes 2.0: The new era of "truth decay". *Just Security.* https://www.justsecurity.org/69677/deepfakes-2-0-the-new-era-of-truth-decay

Jankowicz, N. (2020). *How to lose the information war: Russia, fake news, and the future of conflict.* I.B. Tauris.

Johnson, D. G., & Diakopoulos, N. (2021). What to do about deepfakes? *Communications of the ACM, 64*(3), 33–35.

Joseph, R. (2019). Fakebusters strike back. *Index on Censorship, 48*(1), 76–79.

Kalpokas, I. (2018). *A political theory of post-truth.* Palgrave Macmillan.

Kalpokas, I. (2019). Affective encounters of the algorithmic kind: Post-truth and post-human pleasure. *Social Media + Society.* https://doi.org/10.1177/2056305119845678

Kalpokas, I. (2021a). *Malleable, digital, and posthuman: A permanently beta life.* Emerald.

Kalpokas, I. (2021b). Leadership and agency in algorithmic society. In E. K. Duruk, S. Mengu, & E. Ulusoy (Eds.), *Digital Siege* (pp. 119–140). Istanbul University Press.

Kalpokas, I. (2021c). Problematising reality: The promises and perils of synthetic media. *SN Social Sciences, 1*(1), 1–11.

Kerner, C., & Risse, M. (2021). Beyond porn and discreditation: Epistemic promises and perils of deepfake technology in digital lifeworlds. *Moral Philosophy and Politics, 8*(1), 81–108.

Kikerpill, K. (2020). Choose your stars and studs: The rise of deepfake designer porn. *Porn Studies, 7*(4), 352–356.

Koenig, A. (2019). Half the truth is often a great lie: Deep fakes, open source information, and international criminal law. *American Journal of International Law, 113,* 250–255.

Lyons, B. A., Merola, V., & Reifler, J. (2021). How bad is the fake news problem? The role of baseline information in public perceptions. In R. Greifeneder et al. (Eds.), *The psychology of fake news: Accepting, sharing, and correcting misinformation* (pp. 11–26). Routledge.

Maddalena, G., & Gili, G. (2020). *The history and theory of post-truth communication.* Palgrave Macmillan.

Maddocks, S. (2020). 'A deepfake plot intended to silence me': Exploring continuities between pornographic and 'Political' deep fakes. *Porn Studies, 7*(4), 415–423.

Maras, M.-H., & Alexandrou, A. (2019). Determining authenticity of video evidence in the age of artificial intelligence and in the wake of deepfake videos. *The International Journal of Evidence and Proof, 23*(3), 255–262.

Mazarr, M. J., Bauer, R. M., Casey, A., Heintz, S. A., & Matthews, L. J. (2019). *The emerging risk of virtual societal warfare: Social manipulation in a changing information environment.* The RAND Corporation.

McPeak, A. (2021). The threat of deepfakes in litigation: Raising the authentication bar to combat falsehood. *Vanderbilt Journal of Entertainment and Technology Law, 23*(2), 433–450.

Morgan, B. (2021, April 5). What does it mean to be customer-centric in 2021? *Forbes,* https://www.forbes.com/sites/blakemorgan/2021/04/05/what-does-it-mean-to-be-customer-centric-in-2021/?sh=4ac4eb606364

Murphy, G., & Flynn, E. (2021). Deepfake false memories. *Memory.* https://doi.org/10.1080/09658211.2021.1919715

Nagle, A. (2017). *Kill all normies: Online culture wars from 4chan and tumblr to trump and the alt-right.* Zero Books.

Newton, O. B., & Stanfill, M. (2020). My NSFW video has partial occlusion: Deepfakes and the technological production of non-consensual pornography. *Porn Studies, 7*(4), 398–414.

O'Shaughnessy, N. (2020). From disinformation to fake news: Forwards into the past. In P. Baines, N. O'Shaughnessy, & N. Snow (Eds.), *The SAGE handbook of propaganda* (pp. 55–70). SAGE.

Patersman, T., & Hanley, L. (2020). Political warfare in the digital age: Cyber subversion, information operations and 'Deep Fakes'. *Australian Journal of International Affairs, 74*(4), 439–454.

Paul, C., & Posard, M. N. (2020). Artificial intelligence and the manufacturing of reality. *The RAND Blog,* https://www.rand.org/blog/2020/01/artificial-intelligence-and-the-manufacturing-of-reality.html

Popova, M. (2020). Deepfakes: An introduction. *Porn Studies, 7*(4), 350–351.

Reid, S. (2021). The deepfake dilemma: Reconciling privacy and first amendment protections. *University of Pennsylvania Journal of Constitutional Law, 23*(1), 209–237.

Rizzo, G. L. C., De Marco, M., De Rosa, P., & Laura, L. (2020). Collaborative recommendations with deep feed-forward networks: An approach to service personalization. In H. Nóvoa, M. Drăgoicea, & N. Kühl (Eds.), *Exploring service science* (pp. 65–78). Springer.

Schick, N. (2020). *Deep fakes and the infocalypse: What you urgently need to know.* Monoray.

Seo, H. (2020). Visual propaganda and social media. In P. Baines, N. O'Shaughnessy, & N. Snow (Eds.), *The SAGE handbook of propaganda* (pp. 126–136). SAGE.

Shah, D., & Murthi, B. P. S. (2021). Marketing in a data-driven world: Implications for the role and scope of marketing. *Journal of Business Research, 21*, 772–779.

Simonite, T. (2019, September 4). Forget politics: For now, deepfakes are for bullies. *Wired,* https://www.wired.com/story/forget-politics-deepfakes-bullies/

Solsman, J. E. (2019, May 24). Samsung deepfake AI could fabricate a video of you from a single profile pic. *CNET,* https://www.cnet.com/news/samsung-ai-deepfake-can-fabricate-a-video-of-you-from-a-single-photo-mona-lisa-cheapfake-dumbfake/

Susskind, J. (2018). *Future politics: Living together in a world transformed by tech.* Oxford University Press.

Thomas, E. (2019, November 25). In the battle against deepfakes, AI is pitted against AI. *Wired,* https://www.wired.co.uk/article/deepfakes-ai

Tucker, P. (2020, August 6). Deepfakes are getting better, easier to make, and cheaper. *Defense One,* https://www.defenseone.com/technology/2020/08/deepfakes-are-getting-better-easier-make-and-cheaper/167536/

Vaccari, C., & Chadwick, A. (2020). Deepfakes and disinformation: Exploring the impact of synthetic political video on deception, uncertainty, and trust in news. *Social Media + Society.* https://doi.org/10.1177/2056305120903408

Venkataramakrishnan, S. (2019, October 24). Can you believe your eyes? How deepfakes are coming for politics. *Financial Times*, https://www.ft.com/content/4bf4277c-f527-11e9-a79c-bc9acae3b654

Wahl-Jorgensen, K., & Carlson, M. (2021). Conjecturing fearful futures: Journalistic discourses on deepfakes. *Journalism Practice*. https://doi.org/10.1080/17512786.2021.1908838

Weinstein, A. (2020). Creating superior customer value in the now economy. *Journal of Creating Value, 6*(1), 20–33.

Whittaker, L., Letheren, K., & Mulcahy, R. (2021). The rise of deepfakes: A conceptual framework and research agenda for marketing. *Australasian Marketing Journal*. https://doi.org/10.1177/1839334921999479

Whittaker, L., Kietzmann, T. C., Kietzmann, J., & Dabirian, A. (2020). 'All Around Me Are Synthetic Faces': The mad world of AI-generated media. *IT Professional, 22*(5), 90–99.

Wild, J. (2021). Beyond data: The mindsets and disciplines needed to fuel growth. *Journal of Marketing, 85*(1), 190–195.

Wilkerson, L. (2021). Still waters run deep(fakes): The rising concerns of 'Deepfake' technology and its influence on democracy and the first amendment. *Missouri Law Review, 86*(1), 407–432.

Wojewidka, J. (2020). The deepfake threat to face biometrics. *Biometric Technology Today, 2*, 5–7.

Woolley, S. (2020). *The reality game: How the next wave of technology will break the truth and what we can do about it*. Endeavour.

Woolley, S., & Joseff, K. (2020). Demand for deceit: How the way we think drives disinformation. *National Endowment for Democracy and International Forum for Democratic Studies*, https://www.ned.org/wp-content/uploads/2020/01/Demand-for-Deceit.pdf

Yin, X., & Hassner, T. (2021, June 16). Reverse engineering generative models from a single deepfake image. *Facebook AI*, https://ai.facebook.com/blog/reverse-engineering-generative-model-from-a-single-deepfake-image/

Young, N. (2019). *Deepfake technology: Complete guide to deepfakes, politics and social media*. Independently published.

Yu, S. H. (2021, July 19). The First rule of personalization: How to not annoy the customer. *AdWeek*, https://www.adweek.com/performance-marketing/the-first-rule-of-personalization-how-to-not-annoy-the-customer/

Chapter 6
I CAN Do It: From GANs and Deepfakes to Art

Since GANs are effective in generating new data from existing examples, the natural question to ask is whether they represent a new step forward in machine creativity. To some extent, a certain (albeit limited and tightly circumscribed) idea of creativity is already central to machine learning in general—after all, at its heart 'is the idea that an algorithm can be created that will find new questions to ask if it gets something wrong'—by learning from past mistakes, the algorithm tweaks itself so that it produces a better outcome next time (Du Sautoy, 2020a, pp. 67–68). If displayed by human, such quality would likely be called creative thinking. Such ability is particularly acute in deep learning, which effectively involves the 'rewiring' of the entire neural network (or segments thereof) in the process, with such adaptability already manifesting the seeds of creativity within it.

Even more pertinently, it transpires that not only GANs but also the human brain has two distinct forces at play: on one side is 'an exhibitionist urge to make things. To create. To express' while on the other is 'an inhibitor, the critical alter ego that casts doubt on our ideas, that questions and criticises them'; it is only a healthy balance between those two that can ensure a smooth creative process and healthy participation in the society at large (Du Sautoy, 2020a, p. 134). In this sense, the creative aspect inherent to GANs manifests itself in that 'no *extra* data is provided to the system beyond the original training set, yet GANs are able to *extend* the conceptual space of the training set', ultimately displaying 'a more open-ended imaginative processes where novel outputs might be generated' (Bown, 2021, pp. 183; 190). Indeed, at least within certain domains, GANs have quickly become entrenched as creative tools of choice (Tsiaras, 2019). Nevertheless, as shown below, problems in ascribing creativity to GANs (or other digital actors) do arise upon more careful consideration.

Narrowing the discussion down towards GANs necessitates answering the question whether deepfakes are truly creative. On first impression, it might seem tempting to answer in the affirmative: after all, GAN's are creating audiovisual material that had never existed by taking real-world training examples and producing something new—in that sense, one could say, '[t]he amazing thing about GANs is the fact

I. Kalpokas, J. Kalpokiene, *Deepfakes*, SpringerBriefs in Political Science,
https://doi.org/10.1007/978-3-030-93802-4_6

that they actually allow computers and machines to be creative' (Bhanji, 2018); almost identically, for Cascone (2017) 'there may be real artist potential in the world of deep neural networks'. On a somewhat less bombastic note, according to (Miller, 2019), GANs can be seen to imbue AI with something akin to imagination. The latter assertion is, however, debatable. Mere generation of new data would seem insufficient to justify assertions of creativity or imagination. Unsurprisingly, therefore, other authors are more nuanced, stressing that GANs only 'can generate images with new contents from the data distribution learned in the training stage' (Chen et al., 2020). Even more scathingly, Hughes et al. (2021, p. 4) pinpoint that '[a]n optimally trained GAN generator should recreate the training distribution and therefore cannot directly generate an image based on new governing principles' since ultimately only things that are similar to the training data are within a GAN's reach. Almost identically, for Ziska (2019, p. 788), GANs 'do not generate anything creative in their current form' for the reason that 'they are set up to produce works which look like already existing art'—even providing that it is art that they are after (Ziska, 2019, p. 788). In this way, it seems reasonable to conclude that GANs are 'emulative and not creative' (Elgammal et al., 2017, p. 5), thereby diminishing at least some of the early hype around the technology.

Some of the tasks GANs can be used for are relatively easy to set up but are not particularly creative. These could involve reproducing paintings in a different style or rendering one type of image (such as a photo) into a painting 'in the style of' a particular painter. Another potential use relates to the personalisation trend already discussed in different contexts: for example, should you want to have your portrait painted in the style of Da Vinci's *Salvator Mudi*, this could be easily algorithmically arranged, making you your own personal Jesus (probably in more ways than one). Moreover, GAN-produced art has already enjoyed some commercial success, most notably with the *Portrait of Edmond de Bellamy*, generated by a GAN trained on Western portraiture, selling for $432,500 at Christie's. At the very least, the generative capacity unleashed by deep learning algorithms represent democratisation of creativity: as Bown (2021, p. 300) observes, '[i]n the spirit of Instagram filters, the idea that everyone can create *beautiful* things cheaply and easily can be taken forward in obvious ways by computational creativity technology'. Just as it was the photographic and video deepfakes, the opening up of the pool of opportunities and capacities may have a transformative effect—for better or worse. Still, that seems to be significantly more mundane than the grand (or dystopian, depending on whom you ask) visions of machine creativity.

Nevertheless, significantly more creative promise pertains to a variation of GANs—Creative Adversarial Networks, or CANs; it fact, it is possible to claim that CANs represent a shift towards true innovation and inventiveness on behalf of neural networks (Elgammal et al., 2017, p. 5). Hence, CANs represent another improvement by 'driving the network to generate images explicitly *outside* of the training set while (in principle) maintaining the coherence of images' (Bown, 2021, pp. 190–191). The network itself was trained on more than 80,000 artworks spanning 500 years of art (admittedly, Western art only) without curating for specific styles or genres—after all, studying art history is what artists usually do before developing their own distinctive style (Mazzone & Elgammal, 2019, p. 4; see also Elgammal et al., 2017). In this sense, the training of the discriminator on CAN is 'somewhat like an artist taking an art history survey course, with no particular focus on a style or genre' (Elgammal, 2019), bringing it closer to how humans learn about—and subsequently create—art. Just as it is the case with GANs, the generator here is producing new content items, this time—artwork candidates. The difference, however, is with the discriminator that acts as 'an algorithmic art historian that would appraise the output' (Du Sautoy, 2020a, p. 134), penalising the artwork candidates for not just being too far but also for coming *too close* to the training data set. In this way, two opposing forces work simultaneously in CANs, 'one that urges the machine to follow the aesthetics of the art it is shown [. . .], while the other force penalizes the machine if it emulates an already established style [. . .]'; there-fore, the network becomes creative but in a way that is still recognisable by the human audience as 'the art generated will be novel but at the same time will not depart too much from acceptable aesthetic standards' (Mazzone & Elgammal, 2019, p. 3). This idea of creativity is based on Martindale's (1990) 'principle of least effort': artists challenge existing conventions to create fresh and intriguing work but only minimally so in order not to provoke audience aversion. Under this principle, a successful artwork will require the least possible perceptive effort from the audience while simultaneously going beyond boring. In this sense, the dual criticism of the CAN's discriminator can be said to optimise the output's arousal potential (Elgammal et al., 2017; Elgammal, 2019).

The principle can also be illustrated by the so-called Wundt curve, representing the arousal (positive or negative) caused by an artwork where the x axis represents distance from existing artistic canon while the y axis represents hedonic value (both positive and negative): a work that is too familiar is boring and fails to generate much arousal while a work that is too new often seems disconcerting or too difficult to understand, therefore causing negative hedonic value. The peak of *positive* hedonic value, in the meantime, lies at the point of optimal balance between the similar and the new: still recognisable, but beyond boring—for this reason, the discriminator's task is to push the generator towards creating new work that aims for the peak of the Wundt curve (see e.g. Du Sautoy, 2020a, pp. 139–140). By not merely building on training data but by design going beyond it, CANs make it possible to produce works that are 'novel and therefore creative'—indeed 'something altogether new and original' (Miller, 2019, p. 115). Indeed, for Bown (2021, p. 158), '[a] combination of generation and evaluation tasks is key to creative processes'. Hence, there definitely is a fine line here: on the one hand, as Miller (2019, p. 311) observes, computer-generated artworks are often 'of a sort that has never been seen before or even imagined'; clearly, such art 'transcends the merely weird to encompass works that we might consider pleasing and that many artists judge as acceptable'. Seen in this light, CANs seem to represent an improvement in the sense that they are designed not to completely emulate the training data. On the other hand, though, aiming to aesthetically please is not necessarily a sign of creativity—instead, art history shows that it is typically vice versa (Ziska, 2019, p. 789). Likewise, CANs are still as context-unaware as their predecessors: after all, as Elgammal et al. (2017,

p. 21) admit in their paper that introduced this new network type, CAN 'does not have any semantic understanding of art behind the concept of styles', likewise, '[i]t does not know anything about subject matter, or explicit models of elements or principle of art'—all it does is rearranging a set of data points in a particular way that fits within its adversarial model. The same matter is also raised by both Doctorow (2019) and (Bown, 2021), for whom the issue is that the artificial agent knows neither the genres nor the specific cultural context in question. However, one might rather provocatively ask what if the AI agent as such was to be taken as the new cultural context.

Nevertheless, CANs (and, with a little bit of conceptual stretching, GANs as well) do constitute part of what is more generally known as computer-generated art. The latter can be broadly defined as '*the artwork results of some computer program being left to run by itself, with minimal or zero interference from a human being*' (Boden 2012, p. 141). There are plenty of those who would actively question whether such autonomous machinic creativity is possible in principle, not even as a matter of extant technology. This has come to be known as 'the Lovelace objection' after the computing pioneer Ada Lovelace who famously asserted that a machine could ever do only what it was told to do. To this effect, Du Sautoy (2020b, pp. 7–8), for example, employs what he calls a Lovelace test, whereby in order to pass, 'an algorithm must originate a creative work of art such that the process is repeatable (i.e. it isn't the result of a hardware error) and yet the programmer is unable to explain how the algorithm produced its output'. In this way, one would account for activity which is both systematically creative and independently so. Here the distinction between two types of machine learning is crucial: in supervised learning, humans set the rules for creative processes, meaning that it still remains the domain the domain of AI-as-a tool, and not of creativity, by definition unable to pass the Lovelace test. However, with *unsupervised* learning, things become rather more complicated as such algorithms tend to learn in a way reminiscent of how humans do: by observing the world and adjusting any misperceptions. In this way, creativity becomes possible at least in theory. Indeed, as stressed by Mazzone and Elgammal (2019, p. 1), contrary to simple algorithmic art that that had involved specific preprograming of rules and aesthetics, with CANs and other unsupervised learning techniques 'algorithms are set up by the artists to "learn" the aesthetics by looking at many images using machine learning technology', enabling the generation of new output that follow the aesthetics thus learned. Arriagada (2020, p. 401) is similarly optimistic, equating the fact that '[a] CAN is capable of creating and evaluating on its own' with the assertion that such capacity demonstrates 'that a CAN does grow and evolve aesthetically' (Arriagada, 2020, p. 401). While this productive growth and aesthetic evolution can be broadly accepted for fact, the necessary question is where this particular trajectory is taking us and whether true creativity is in sight.

Still, when we come to creative works (or something akin to them) being produced by machine learning tools, the question of whether, after all, it is true creative behaviour remains unanswered in any satisfactory fashion. One of the canonical takes on the matter is by Margaret Boden. For her, '[c]reativity is the ability to come up with ideas or artefacts that are *new, surprising, and valuable'* (Boden 2012, p. 29; see also Boden, 2016, p. 67). In fact, even inasmuch as human creativity is concerned, questions as to its features and recognition abound, making it even more difficult to come up with ways to simulate it on a machine (Boden, 2016, p. 67). She also distinguishes between 'psychological' and 'historical' kinds of creativity, with the former relating to the person (something that is new or surprising to the creating person and the latter pertaining to novelty at a grand scale—something that nobody has come up with before (Boden 2012, p. 30); the latter, obviously, is seen as deserving greater prominence. Another key feature that Boden notes is the capacity of artists to not only recognise rules and create accordingly but also to break out of the 'bubble of fine art' by breaking established conventions, either as an act of rebellion or in order to create new aesthetic forms (Boden 2012, p. 124). Arguably, such 'rebelliousness' might be problematic in the field of AI creativity, although the adversarial underpinning of CANs arguably comes as close as currently technologically possible. Simultaneously, though, one must also keep in mind Du Sautoy (2020b, p. 13) observation that '[c]reativity is not an absolute but a relative activity', whereby '[w]e are creative within our culture and frame of reference'. For this reason, it might be inherently problematic to apply our current views about creativity (which have significantly evolved over centuries) to set an *absolute* standard for artificial creativity.

Regardless of one's take on creativity, it appears to be uncontroversial that autonomy is a key feature. Following Boden (2012, p. 181), autonomy can be seen as comprising of three different dimensions: the first of these pertains to 'the extent to which response to the environment is direct (determined only by the present state of the external world) or indirect (mediated by inner mechanisms that depend in part on the system's previous history)'; the second one denotes 'the extent to which the control mechanisms were self-generated rather than centrally imposed; finally, the third one concerns the capacity for inner reflection upon the mechanisms of direction or their modification in light of broader context and field of concerns. All of those qualities seem to be extremely difficult for an artificial agent, such as a neural network, to achieve. Nevertheless, upon deeper reflection, such a radically self-deterministic take on autonomy would render doubtful an absolute majority of human creative endeavours, particularly where the author has had artistic training and is a socially and culturally engaged person and, therefore, externally affected (if not largely determined) by both the artistic tradition and socio-cultural norms. Such unavoidable involvement of multiple factors and influences in the creative process is well-encapsulated in the embedded and distributed understanding of creativity advocated by Bown (2021).

Nevertheless, questions of agency abound. As Du Sautoy (2020a, p. 105) observes, '[c]reativity is ultimately an expression of human free will, and until computers have their own version of this, art created by a computer will always be traceable back to a human desire to create' (Du Sautoy, 2020a, p. 105). Likewise, for Benedikter (2021, p. 84), art, 'whichever way we define it, is and remains tied to the human will in its core: to the *will of creation* which [. . .] is still exclusive to humans'. For Miller (2019, p. 265), meanwhile, the major obstacle standing between machines and proper creativity is their lack of awareness—although CANs probably come as close to that as realistically possible given today's technology as a result of their competitive nature and the discriminator's specific optimisation brief. Nevertheless, as admitted by Elgammal and colleagues in a quote above, that still remains superficial awareness, one without real understanding of the underlying concepts and ideas. Similarly, according to Bown (2021, p. 36), for an artificial agent to go beyond mere generation, it needs to have the capacity for self-evaluation, meaning that 'the system not only generates possible artefacts but applies judgement over their quality'. Again, CANs push at the boundary by being explicitly designed to exercise that kind of judgement. Still, however, that might not be enough because '[h]uman reflexivity involves being able to generate not only new possible outputs but also new methods, goals, and conceptualizations' (Bown, 2021, p. 38)—something artificial creative agents are generally lacking.

Indeed, much of what is produced by machines can be seen as falling into the category of 'mere generation', i.e. production of 'artefacts with the formal properties of a given class, such as 'poem-shaped texts or cantata-shaped sounds'; in order to go beyond, it needs 'a capacity for self-critique and the ability to rank and filter its own well-formed outputs by quality' without there being a human in the loop (Veale & Pérez y Pérez, 2020, p. 556). Arguably, the dual discriminator of a CAN does provide such function. Still, it is also correct that '[e]ven if the network is able to depart from existing styles, this does not mean that the network is able to generate its own distinct style' instead of generating output that is stylistically and aesthetically ambiguous or otherwise indeterminate; hence, while the resulting outcome may be creative (and could quite likely be such), there is still need to take a further step from ambiguity to the development and systematic adoption of a unique style, akin to the signature style of a human artist (Ziska, 2019, p. 791). However, there is a further obstacle that neither CANs nor any other artificially creative agents seem to be able to overcome, at least as of now—it is the need for 'a sense of form and a sense of how form conveys meaning' (Veale & Pérez y Pérez, 2020, p. 557). Indeed, the sense of *meaning* is arguably among the hardest (if not *the* hardest) to achieve, at least as long as algorithmic creation of artworks is concerned, in principle, with the sorting and arrangement of data points as opposed to holistic conceptual thinking—but that would, possibly necessitate venturing into the domain of Artificial General Intelligence, i.e., from the standpoint of current technology, science fiction.

A related challenge raised by researchers and commentators alike is that AI is incapable of interacting with the broader social and cultural context (Svedman, 2020). In other words, it is asserted that contrary to human authors, AI is incapable of taking societal and cultural conditions into account and taking a stance vis-à-vis them or relating to the audience in a particular way. That, however, is an odd observation to make in times of pervasive datafication. Not only taking the entire world as data for purposes of mining and sense-making is the standard practice of today (see, among others, Couldry & Mejias, 2019; Zuboff, 2019) but also AI artists have been developed to adapt their style and 'mood' considering the prevalent sentiments mined from the news of the day (Miller, 2019, p. 123). In that sense, provided sufficient data on the aspects considered relevant, AI artists could probably be even better placed than humans to tap into social, political, and even artistic tendencies and antinomies of the day. Whether, to what extent, and under what conditions such access should be granted to commercial creative AI is a separate, and controversial, issue (see e.g. Lim, 2018; Degli Eposti et al., 2020; Gervais, 2020; Senftleben & Buijtelaar, 2020).

Moreover, it is also the case that humans and computers see the world in ways that are vastly different (Miller, 2019, p. 268). In case of artistic endeavours, for example, humans are concerned with the barely graspable (and barely, if at all, codifiable) drives for expression of emotion, feeling, or some inner view of the world; meanwhile, machines operate in terms of optimising and arranging into emergent patterns the data points available, without any conception of the inner (and with only task-specific conception of the outer) world, let alone expressive drives. Nevertheless, regardless of where we set the bar for creative works proper (and whether we are ready to accept the very possibility of algorithmic creativity), it is already clear that digital agents are already 'emulating humans and laying siege to what has been a strictly human outpost: intellectual creativity' (Gervais, 2020, p. 2057). At the very least, one must acknowledge the 'ambiguity' in the creative relationship between humans and machines, signalling a shift from mere 'interaction' to 'convergence' of humans and machines in artistic creation (Benedikter, 2021, pp. 46, 76).

One thing is clear, however—creativity (or, at the very least, the 'art-ness' of the resulting output) is impossible without audience involvement: as noted by Du Sautoy (2020a, p. 204), 'it is the listener who brings their emotions to the music. The role of the listener, viewer or reader in creating a work of art is often underestimated'. In terms of public acclaim, though, virtuality does not seem to be an issue—in some cases, it might even add an extra layer of attraction (Miller, 2019). In fact, there is good reason to go much further—as, for example, Moruzzi (2020) asserts, 'creativity' is a deeply anthropocentric concept that typically involves the conviction of human exclusivity. Under this paradigm, any instance where 'artificial entities instantiate behaviors and activities that are typical of creative agents, is perceived as dishonest or, even more drastically, it triggers uncomfortable feelings of rejection and discontent' (Moruzzi, 2020, p. 95). It seems to be fair to say that, among other issues, machine-generated art, at least to some extent, has a perception problem, being seen as cold and impersonal, as opposed to the perceived warmth of human art (Kawai, 2020). On the other hand, in blind surveys audiences seem to find it hard to tell art generated by artificial neural networks from human-created or even rank the former higher; that should not come as a surprise given that CANs, as showed above, are explicitly designed to aesthetically please (Trehan, 2021). The latter capacity is likely to be particularly important as artificial creativity will, most probably, not lead to art for its own sake. If the trajectory of the usage of other digital optimising tools is anything to go by in predicting the future uptake and use of artificial creativity, the main, and most influential, adopters will likely be some of the major digital platforms and technology companies; in this way, AI creativity may lead to a future where artistic endeavours become 'inextricable from the same platforms that run the information economy and all its newly potent political apparatuses' (Pepi, 2020). That definitely seems to be a chilling prospect for *both* art and society in general.

References

Arriagada, L. (2020). CG-art: Demystifying the anthropocentric bias of artistic creativity. *Connection Science, 32*(4), 398–405.

Benedikter, R. (2021). Can machines create art? A "Hot" topic for the future of commodified art markets. *Challenge, 64*(1), 75–86.

Bhanji, Z. (2018, December 7). Generative adversarial networks: Can AI be creative? *Medium*, https://medium.com/@zaynahbhanji/generative-adversarial-networks-can-ai-be-creative-47a7c90181ad

Boden, M. (2012). *Creativity and art: Three roads to surprise*. Oxford University Press.

Boden, M. (2016). *AI: Its nature and future*. Oxford University Press.

Bown, O. (2021). *Beyond the creative species: Making machines that make art and music*. The MIT Press.

Cascone, S. (2017, July 11). AI-generated art now looks more convincingly human than work at art basel, study says. *ArtNet*, https://news.artnet.com/art-world/rutgers-artificial-intelligence-art-1019066

Chen, H., Zhao, L., Qiu, L., Wang, Z., Zhang, H., Xing, W., et al. (2020). Creative and diverse artwork generation using adversarial networks. *IET Computer Vision, 14*(8), 650–657.

Couldry, N., & Mejias, U. A. (2019). *The costs of connection: How data is colonizing human life and appropriating it for capitalism*. Stanford University Press.

Degli Eposti, M., Lagioia, F., & Sartor, G. (2020). The use of copyrighted works by AI systems: Art works in the data mill. *European Journal of Risk Regulation, 11*(1), 51–69.

Doctorow, C. (2019, March 9). Creative adversarial networks: GANs that make art. *Boing Boing*, https://boingboing.net/2019/03/09/novelty-discerner.html

Du Sautoy, M. (2020a). *The creativity code: Art and innovation in the age of AI*. The Belknap Press of Harvard University Press.

Du Sautoy, M. (2020b). *The creativity code: How AI is learning to write, paint and think*. 4th Estate.

Elgammal, A. (2019). AI is blurring the definition of artist. *American Scientist, 107*(1) https://www.americanscientist.org/article/ai-is-blurring-the-definition-of-artist

Elgammal, A., Liu, B., Elhoseiny, M., & Mazzone, M. (2017). CAN: Creative adversarial networks generating "Art" by learning about styles and deviating from style norms. *arXiv*, https://arxiv.org/abs/1706.07068

Gervais, D. J. (2020). The machine as author. *Iowa Law Review, 105*, 2053–2106.

Hughes, R. T., Zhu, L., & Bednarz, T. (2021). Generative adversarial networks-enabled human-artificial intelligence collaborative applications for creative and design industries: A systematic review of approaches and trends. *Frontiers in Artificial Intelligence, 4*, 1–17.

Kawai, H. (2020, August 2). Creative Adversarial Networks (CAN) and artificial intelligence as artist. *Medium*, https://medium.com/can-artificial-intelligence-can-be-an-artist/creative-adversarial-networks-can-and-artificial-intelligence-as-artist-fd8a33181c33

Lim, D. (2018). AI & IP: Innovation & creativity in an age of accelerated change. *Akron Law Review, 52*(3), 813–876.

Martindale, C. (1990). *The clockwork muse: The predictability of artistic change*. Basic Books.

Mazzone, M., & Elgammal, A. (2019). Art, creativity, and the potential of artificial intelligence. *Arts, 8*(1), 1–9.

Miller, A. (2019). *The artist in the machine: The World of AI-powered creativity*. The MIT Press.

Moruzzi, C. (2020). Artificial creativity and general intelligence. *Journal of Science and Technology of the Arts, 12*(3), 84–99.

Pepi, M. (2020, May 6). How does a human critique art made by AI? *Art News*, https://www.
    artnews.com/art-in-america/features/creative-ai-art-criticism-1202686003/
Senftleben, M., & Buijtelaar, L. (2020). Robot creativity: An incentive-based neighboring rights
    approach. *European Intellectual Property Review, 42*(12), 717–740.
Svedman, M. (2020). Artificial creativity: A case against copyright for AI-created visual artwork. *IP
    Theory, 9*(1), 1–22.
Trehan, D. (2021, March 8). Digital artist: Creative Adversarial Networks (CAN). *Towards AI*,
    https://towardsai.net/p/latest/digital-artist-creative-adversarial-networkscan
Tsiaras, T. (2019, January 22). Generative adversarial networks – When AI gets creative. *The Data
    Lab*, https://www.thedatalab.com/tech-blog/generative-adversarial-networks-when-ai-gets-
    creative/
Veale, T., & Pérez y Pérez, R. (2020). Leaps and bounds: An introduction to the field of
    computational creativity. *New Generation Computing, 38*, 551–563.
Ziska, J. D. (2019). Artificial creativity and generative adversarial networks. *Proceedings of the
    European Society for Aesthetics, 11*, 781–796.
Zuboff, S. (2019). *The age of surveillance capitalism: The fight for a human future at the new
    frontier of power*. Profile Books.

Chapter 7
Regulation: Public, Private, Autonomous?

Deepfakes are described as a dual-use technology by the European Parliamentary Research Service (2021, p. 70), and there is a good reason for seeing them in this way: despite of the benefits they may bring, there are also multiple threats to both individual persons and whole societies. This chapter will focus on three modalities of regulation: law, platform policies, and technological solutions, such as automatic detection. As shown below, current legal regulation is often insufficient or wholly inadequate, meaning that private regulation by online platforms transpires to be the most efficient regulatory measure available. However, such regulation is not uniform in either substance or application. Moreover, it must be stressed that due to the amount of content that has to be dealt with, such regulation can only be effective if it is automated; while such automation has obvious efficiency benefits, as demonstrated, potential vulnerabilities are present as well.

A useful inspiration for conceptualising potential dimensions of regulation could be Majid Yar's longstanding effort to explain cybercrime by using Routine Activity Theory, or RAT for short (see Yar, 2005; Leukfeldt & Yar, 2016). This approach takes the perpetrators to be rational actors who make their decisions on the basis of target characteristics and the presence of capable guardianship (or lack thereof). In other words, perpetrators are not just mere opportunists who randomly jump in on a target but, in fact, utility maximisers who routinely engage in activities that offer the best outcomes. However, as Yar (2005) notes, one should not limit the analysis to the narrowly economic take on rationality—other units of utility calculation, such as emotional rewards, should be taken into account as well. The characteristics of targets that matter in a RAT approach include value, inertia, visibility, and accessibility. The more *valuable* the target (the more satisfaction gained from deepfake porn, the more material gains to be obtain from defrauding or blackmailing a victim or commercialising their digitised likeness, the more consequential is the destruction of somebody's reputation), the more likely the perpetrator is to engage in the activity; as for *inertia*, the more easily movable the target is, the more attractive it becomes—and when one deals with attributes like (self-) gratification, reputation, or informational influence, virtually no inertia is encountered. Then, when it comes to

I. Kalpokas, J. Kalpokiene, *Deepfakes*, SpringerBriefs in Political Science,
https://doi.org/10.1007/978-3-030-93802-4_7

visibility, awareness of potential targets increases the likelihood that they will be chosen and since today's online environment thrives on visibility, one is targetable essentially by design; *accessibility*, meanwhile, relates to the environmental and contextual characteristics that make the perpetrators aims more or less easy to achieve, which, taking into account the availability of digital content on most individuals for use as training data (and even more so for high-profile targets) and the presence of effective distribution channels should they be necessary (as in disinformation or synthetic pornography for harassment purposes, or selling digital commercial works featuring the victim's likeness), should be taken as high by default (for a discussion of the four characteristics, albeit in connection with regular cybercrime, see Yar, 2005, pp. 419–422; Leukfeldt & Yar, 2016, pp. 269–271). Finally, capable guardianship means the presence of any potential protections, from the victims' self-protective abilities and any private individuals capable of coming to help to law enforcement (see, again, Yar, 2005; Leukfeldt & Yar, 2016).

Particularly as a result of the alarmist discourse outlined earlier in this book, there is an increasing push to act upon 'the intentional, deleterious application of deepfake technology' and regulate its use (Kirchengast, 2020, p. 309). Indeed, as Pradhan (2020) rather dramatically puts it, '[a] flat-out ban on deepfakes seems to be the most effective way to eliminate all the problems'. Nevertheless, it is also clear that something has to be done: while an outright ban on deepfakes would be imprudent due to the multiple beneficial (or, at least, neutral) uses, the threats that deepfakes pose demand a uniform and effective law that punishes harmful use of deepfakes and deters prospective bad actors' (Langa, 2021, p. 769). Still, this is often easier said than done: for example, particularly in the US, many deepfakes would allegedly fall under First Amendment protection (Kirchengast, 2020, p. 309). Pradhan (2020) also admits that a ban 'would violate the conception of freedom of expression as a fundamental individual right'. This, however, is not just a First Amendment matter for the US—freedom of expression is entrenched (albeit, admittedly, less absolutely) in both global human rights documents (such as the Universal Declaration of Human Rights and the International Covenant on Civil and Political Rights) and regional human rights regimes (Pradhan, 2020). Ways to tackle and take down deepfakes through indirect means, for example through recourse to copyright law, are also limited as deepfakes would likely be considered transformative work (in the US) or fall under similar copyright exceptions elsewhere (Reid, 2021, pp. 220–221). Meanwhile, according to Kikerpill (2020, p. 354) '[a]s a matter of civil recourse, beefing up applicable privacy and data protection laws is a step towards the positive, but it would be naïve to assume such developments will prompt fundamental changes'— after all, '[i]f that was the case, online avenues would have ceased to be flooded with pirated content long ago'.

Even in cases when the harm caused by deepfakes appears to be obvious, victims can often find it extremely difficult to put the perpetrators to account. That is the case, notably, with non-consensual deepfake pornography. Even when laws against 'revenge porn' exist, they are unlikely to help because the actual body of the victim (except for the face) is not shown (Reid, 2021, pp. 224–225; see also Harris, 2018; Gieseke, 2020); moreover, in the US, the pornographic nature of such synthetic recordings would not suffice unless the content is deemed obscene, particularly if specific laws against non-consensual pornography do not exist at a state level (Wilkerson, 2021, p. 418). However, even the latter could be ineffective, again, primarily because the only body part of the victim in the video is their face—at the moment, only a few US states (most notably, Virginia, California, Hawaii, and New York) have specifically legislated against computer-generated non-consensual pornography that also entails an individual's likeness being transposed onto either somebody else's body or completely computer-generated body parts (see Ferraro, 2021; Ferraro & Tompros, 2021; Wilkerson, 2021, pp. 423–424). In the UK, meanwhile, English and Welsh law likewise only prohibits non-consensual porn when real images are being used; Scottish law, however, appears to be more inclusive as it also covers images that have been altered, in whatever way such alteration would occur (Selbie & Williams, 2021).

Of course, a person's likeness can be used for purposes other than pornography. In particular, debates are ongoing as to the use of the likeness of actors and other celebrities, and the ability to licence publicity rights for commercial purposes, such as in films or musical productions (see e.g. Gardner, 2019). However, concerns also extend further, for example, to include the effects that the commercial use of celebrity likeness might have on others—as in forcing aspiring actors out of work if films are primarily populated by digital doppelgangers of A-list celebrities from times present and past (Gardner, 2019). In Schick's (2020, p. 155) view, however, the issue is even more fundamental, though, and is set to become 'a much broader civil-rights problem, as our likeness and our voices are stolen and our rights to privacy and security are consequently undermined'. In this context, New York's legislation that grants a right of publicity to its famous residents whose image is used to create a digital replica or to reproduce a person's likeness in any other way for commercial purposes (unless, of course, such representation falls under First Amendment protections) and extends such right beyond death is seen as trailblazing (Feitel et al., 2020; Ferraro & Tompros, 2021). Under this statute, any such reproduction without the consent of the individual or their heirs is now illegal, unless it is clear to a reasonable observer that this is a digital reproduction or a clear disclaimer is given. However, in this context, one should also consider the ethics of bringing the dead back to life, both in terms of the potential traumatic effect on their relatives and with regards to the deceased obviously no longer having a say about the situations in which they are depicted and the kind of content in which they are featured, particularly if that is something they would have objected to had they still been alive (see e.g. Hanley, 2020).

Some effort is also being put into tackling deepfake-enabled political manipulation (or, at least, the perceived threat thereof). In the US, for example, there is legislation against the use of deepfakes to tamper with elections in Texas and California (Wilkerson, 2021, p. 424; see also Ferraro & Tompros, 2021). At the federal level, the DEEPFAKES Accountability Act was introduced in Congress in 2019, mandating deepfake content to be clearly labelled as such and explicitly prohibiting their use for harassment, humiliation, incitement of violence, fraud, or interference in elections (Pesetski, 2020; Pradhan, 2020; Langa, 2021). In terms of other notable jurisdictions, China, not uncharacteristically, is taking a rather heavy-handed approach on deepfakes. There, since 2020, it is a criminal offence to publish deepfake content without explicit disclosure (De Saulles, 2021; Pradhan, 2020). Meanwhile, UK, for example, does not have any deepfake-specific regulation; hence, the only option that remains to those with a legitimate interest to challenge the production and dissemination of deepfakes is to rely on the general restrictions arising from 'anti-fraud legislation, and protections against harassment, defamation, and copyright infringement, as well as data protection laws' (Graham, 2021). Moreover, when it comes to the specific individuals and their likenesses, it must be kept in mind that 'the UK does not have a specific law protecting a person's "image" or "personality"' with the effect that 'that the subject of a deepfake needs to rely on a hotchpotch of rights that are neither sufficient nor adequate to protect the individual in this situation' (Daniel & O'Flaherty, 2021; see also Elks, 2021). Meanwhile, in countries like Germany, Spain, and France, laws intended to tackle disinformation could be used against certain kinds of deepfakes (Pradhan, 2020). However, deepfakes directed against private persons (as in e.g. deepfake pornography) would not be covered. Having said that, image rights are protected in the case law of the European Court of Human Rights (European Court of Human Rights, 2020; European Parliamentary Research Service, 2021, p. 40). As for the EU, the focus is again on disinformation as a political and public order threat, including guidelines for platform-based takedown of malicious deepfakes (Pradhan, 2020). The current proposal for a new AI Regulation leaves ample room for interpretation as to which risk category deepfakes would belong to—although, paradoxically, algorithms used for *detecting* deepfakes would almost certainly fall under high risk, thus making combating deepfakes more difficult (and more seriously regulated) than creating them (European Parliamentary Research Service, 2021).

An alternative approach that has been floated around is to expand the pool of relevant actors: instead of focusing solely on government regulation, for example, Huston and Bahm (2020) stress that '[i]t will take a whole of society approach where government, academia, and corporations work collaboratively with international partners and individual citizens' in order to tackle the harmful use of deepfakes. Here, the argument goes, an important role should also be played by media outlets and social platforms as '[t]raditional and social media should assess criteria for evaluating suspicious unverified, potential deepfakes that could harm society' (Huston & Bahm, 2020). Indeed, relying on private regulation by online platforms would likely be 'the most feasible short-term solution' (Pradhan, 2020). An identical position is also expressed by the law firm Alston Asquith (2021): for them, 'whilst laws remain non-specific, we currently rely on big tech to make their own rules' (Alston Asquith, 2021). Social media platforms are increasingly assertive against deepfakes, with full or partial bans being imposed on Facebook, Twitter, Instagram, Reddit, and TikTok. However, despite the growing willingness to take a stand against deepfakes, loopholes remain, such as allowing content that is satirical or of relatively poor visual quality (Wilkerson, 2021, pp. 411–412). Also, ambiguity remains as to the attitudes of other representatives of the social media platform economy: Snapchat, for example, is taking a different approach and is investing in deepfake creation technology (De Saulles, 2021) while other platforms appear to be largely indifferent to the malicious activity happening under their watch—Telegram, for example, continues to host deepfake bots, including the infamous 'undressing' apps (Harrar, 2021). Moreover, particularly pornography sites appear to be highly ambiguous in terms of their attempts to combat deepfakes, such as simply filtering for the term being used in the title of uploaded videos and even then not accounting for variations and deliberate misspellings of it (Maddocks, 2020, p. 419). Likewise, proactiveness is often lacking: for example, on Pornhub, while deepfakes are banned, identification remains a challenge (Alston Asquith, 2021).

In order to successfully tackle harmful deepfakes, automatic tools for deepfake detection and video authentication acquire particular importance (Huston & Bahm, 2020). Similar emphasis on forensic algorithms is also clearly visible in a recent report by the European Parliamentary Research Service (2021, p. 7). With the growing accessibility of deepfake production tools, manual moderation becomes an impossibility due to the sheer volume of content, not to mention its sophistication; some iterations of the necessary detection technology already exist, but in all likelihood 'there will be a continuous battle between video creators and social media to play catch up with each other' (Alston Asquith, 2021). Indeed, despite the fact that considerable work is being put by researchers from both academic institutions and private companies into developing techniques for detecting and verifying deepfake content so that their negative effect is minimised, this is, and will remain, a perpetual struggle, since every improvement in detection techniques only serves as an impetus for further innovation by the threat actors or those creating apps for amateur deepfake production (Gosse & Burkell, 2020, p. 498). For this reason, there will always be deepfakes that evade the filters available at the time.

Techniques used for automated deepfake detection involve speaker recognition, to verify the personality of the speaker based on training data; voice liveliness detection to check whether the features and patterns of audio in the recording are commensurable with those of a live human voice; facial recognition to detect distortions to the face of the person allegedly featured in the video; facial feature analysis to search for abnormalities in certain facial landmarks, such as abnormal blinking; a search for temporal inconsistencies, such as sudden shifts in the body or in the background, normally unlikely in nearby frames; examination of visual artefacts, particularly at the edges between the person in the video and the background as deepfake video generation often results in distortion in such areas; and search for authenticity indicators, such as pixel sensitivity variations present in any digitally captured material (European Parliamentary Research Service, 2021, pp. 18–19). However, serious limitations are present as well. For example, such detection tools can only be trained on known deepfakes, which means that innovations in detection evasion will not be accounted for; also, content uploaded on social media is often compressed and distorted in the process, thus significantly shrinking the difference between deepfakes and genuine content (European Parliamentary Research Service, 2021, p. 19). Moreover, it is also not unlikely that a sophisticated threat actor engaging in a high-stakes deepfake disinformation campaign would potentially be capable to foil detection efforts by polluting the training data set with adversarial examples (see Hussain et al., 2021).

Ultimately, it must be admitted, with Johnson and Diakopoulos (2021, p. 33), that in deepfake creation and dissemination processes '[r]esponsibility can be diffuse and ambiguous', not least due to the need to take into consideration 'multiple actors who create the deepfake, develop the tool used to make it, provide the social media platform for amplification, redistribute it, and so on', leaving accountability unclear and jurisdiction difficult to determine (Johnson & Diakopoulos, 2021, p. 33). Regulation (or, rather, enforcement) is also hampered by the anonymity afforded by the internet—some popular platforms (e.g. TikTok) do not require any form of identity verification (Walker, 2021). Moreover, it is also the case that '[o]nce a deepfake is on the Internet, it is likely to be difficult to successfully find and eradicate all copies of the deepfake' that will have spread far and wide, including to platforms that are not bent on compliance (Daniel & O'Flaherty, 2021). That is a common concern for all jurisdictions which, in combination with anonymity, poses a severe challenge even in cases when adequate legislation exists. After all, there is little benefit to regulation if it is unenforceable. For this reason, it is more than likely that the regulation of deepfakes remains a patchwork of initiatives and approaches without significant chances of success. What becomes clear, though, is that the capacity to regulate and control technology, whatever modality such control would assume, has become severely hampered.

References

Alston Asquith. (2021, March 8). Deepfake and the Law, https://www.alstonasquith.com/deepfake-and-the-law/

Daniel, C., & O'Flaherty, A. (2021, March 23). The rise of "Deepfake" demands urgent legal reform in the UK. *The National Law Review*, https://www.natlawreview.com/article/rise-deepfake-demands-urgent-legal-reform-uk

De Saulles, M. (2021, March 26). How deepfakes are a problem for us all and why the law needs to change. *Information Matters*, https://informationmatters.net/deepfakes-problem-why-law-needs-to-change/

Elks, S. (2021, February 26). Sharing 'Deepfake' porn images should be a crime, says British Law Body. *Reuters*, https://www.reuters.com/article/britain-women-lawmaking-idUSL8N2KU7NL

European Court of Human Rights. (2020). *Right to the protection of one's image*, https://www.echr.coe.int/Documents/FS_Own_image_ENG.pdf

European Parliamentary Research Service. (2021). *Tackling deepfakes in European Policy*, https://www.europarl.europa.eu/thinktank/en/document.html?reference=EPRS_STU(2021)690039

Feitel, J., Balin, R. D., & Rosenfeld, J. (2020, December 4). Dead celebrities and digital doppelgangers: New York expands its right of publicity statute and tackles sexually explicit deepfakes. *DWT*, https://www.dwt.com/insights/2020/12/new-york-post-mortem-right-of-publicity

Ferraro, M. F. (2021, June 23). Hawaii outlaws some deepfakes. *The SCIF*, https://thescif.org/hawaii-outlaws-some-deepfakes-d9feaff05b30

Ferraro, M. F., & Tompros, L. W. (2021). New York's right to publicity and deepfakes law breaks new ground. *The Computer & Internet Lawyer, 38*(4), 1–4.

Gardner, E. (2019, July 12). Deepfakes pose increasing legal and ethical issues for hollywood. *The Hollywood Reporter*, https://www.hollywoodreporter.com/business/business-news/deepfakes-pose-increasing-legal-ethical-issues-hollywood-1222978/

Gieseke, A. P. (2020). 'The New Weapon of Choice': Law's current inability to properly address deepfake pornography. *Vanderbilt Law Review, 73*(5), 1479–1516.

Gosse, C., & Burkell, J. (2020). Politics and porn: How news media characterizes problems presented by deepfakes. *Critical Studies in Media Communication, 37*(5), 497–511.

Graham, N. (2021). Deepfake deception: The emerging threat of deepfake attacks. *Dentons*, https://www.dentons.com/en/insights/articles/2021/may/21/deepfake-deception-the-emerging-threat-of-deepfake-attacks

Hanley, J. (2020, November 26). The Ethics of Rebooting the Dead. *Wired*, https://www.wired.com/story/ethics-reviving-dead-with-tech/

Harrar, J. (2021, April 1). Should you believe what your own eyes are seeing? The malicious intent of deepfakes. *Lawyer Monthly*, https://www.lawyer-monthly.com/2021/04/should-you-believe-what-your-own-two-eyes-are-seeing-the-malicious-intent-of-deepfakes/

Harris, D. (2018). Deepfakes: False pornography is here and the law cannot protect you. *Duke Law & Technology Review, 17*, 99–128.

Hussain, S., Neekhara, P., Jere, M., Koushanfar, F., & McAuley, J. (2021). Adversarial deepfakes: Evaluating vulnerability of deepfake detectors to adversarial examples. *2021 IEEE Winter Conference on Applications of Computer Vision (WACV)*. pp. 3347–3356.

Huston, R. P., & Bahm, M. E. (2020, April 14). Deepfakes 2.0: The new era of 'Truth Decay', *Just Security*, https://www.justsecurity.org/69677/deepfakes-2-0-the-new-era-of-truth-decay/

Johnson, D. G., & Diakopoulos, N. (2021). What to do about deepfakes? *Communications of the ACM, 64*(3), 33–35.

Kikerpill, K. (2020). Choose your stars and studs: The rise of deepfake designer porn. *Porn Studies, 7*(4), 352–356.

Kirchengast, T. (2020). Deepfakes and image manipulation: Criminalisation and control. *Information and Telecommunications Technology Law, 29*(3), 308–323.

Langa, J. (2021). Deepfakes, real consequences: Crafting legislation to combat threats posed by deepfakes. *Boston University Law Review, 101*, 761–801.

Leukfeldt, E. R., & Yar, M. (2016). Applying routine activity theory to cybercrime: A theoretical and empirical analysis. *Deviant Behavior, 37*(3), 263–280.

Maddocks, S. (2020). 'A Deepfake Plot Intended to Silence Me': Exploring continuities between pornographic and 'Political' deep fakes. *Porn Studies, 7*(4), 415–423.

Pesetski, A. (2020). Deepfakes: A new content category for a digital age. *William & Mary Bill of Rights Journal, 29*(2), 503–532.

Pradhan, P. (2020, October 4). AI deepfakes: The goose is cooked? *University of Illinois Law Review*, https://www.illinoislawreview.org/blog/ai-deepfakes/

Reid, S. (2021). The deepfake dilemma: Reconciling privacy and first amendment protections. *University of Pennsylvania Journal of Constitutional Law, 23*(1), 209–237.

Schick, N. (2020). *Deep fakes and the infocalypse: What you urgently need to know*. Monoray.

Selbie, T., & Williams, C. (2021, May 27). Deepfake pornography could become epidemic, Expert Warns, *BBC*, https://www.bbc.com/news/uk-scotland-57254636

Walker, W. (2021, March 24). Mission Impossible? The legal implications of managing deepfake celebrity videos. *Harvard Journal of Sports and Entertainment Law*, https://harvardjsel.com/2021/03/mission-impossible-the-legal-implications-of-managing-deepfake-celebrity-videos/

Wilkerson, L. (2021). Still waters run deep(fakes): The rising concerns of 'Deepfake' technology and its influence on democracy and the first amendment. *Missouri Law Review, 86*(1), 407–432.

Yar, M. (2005). The novelty of 'Cybercrime': An assessment in light of routine activity theory. *European Journal of Criminology, 2*(4), 407–427.

Chapter 8
Broader Implications: Politics and Digital Posthumanism

As showed in the previous chapters, deepfakes do have a potential to partake in important societal transformations and to contribute to large-scale and broad-ranging problems and issues that partake to our social and political life, although not necessarily (or not always) in ways predicted by the more alarmist takes on the matter. However, deepfakes, and the underlying technology—GANs and, more broadly, deep learning—cannot be seen in isolation. Instead, they are part and parcel of broader processes involving humans, technology, and the natural environment. Generally speaking, such interrelationships are best analysed from a posthumanist standpoint. Therefore, this chapter is dedicated to wrapping up the analysis of deepfakes and their underlying technologies by pinpointing the way in which they contribute to the broader rejection of ideas around human autonomy and primacy while also questioning ideas around the very possibility of privileged access to reality.

Indeed, one could simply quote from Chandler (2015, p. 850) that '[p] osthumanism is what is says on the tin: it is an assertion that governing the world on the basis of the politics of modernity [. . .] is dangerous, false and hubristic and does nothing to remove the hierarchies, inequalities, injustice and suffering of the world'. It must be admitted that both abstract disembodied reason and rationality, as features distinguishing humans from animals, are specifically and exclusively modern attributes that, among other things, have atomised the social nature of ethics; with the growing independence and agency of technological artefacts, the illusory nature of such anthropocentrism has been underscored particularly clearly (The Onlife Initiative, 2015a, p. 8). This ultimately necessitates facing up to the need for recognising the blurring of the distinction between reality and virtuality and between people, nature, and artefacts (The Onlife Initiative, 2015b, p. 44) to the extent that any distinction between such (and other) categories becomes indeterminate (Lupton, 2020, p. 17). In fact, Braidotti (2019a, p. 47), for example, goes even further by underscoring as the key assumption of her own version of the posthumanist project the idea that 'all matter or substance is one and immanent to itself', ultimately meaning that 'the posthuman subject asserts the material totality of

© The Author(s), under exclusive license to Springer Nature Switzerland AG 2022   73
I. Kalpokas, J. Kalpokiene, *Deepfakes*, SpringerBriefs in Political Science,
https://doi.org/10.1007/978-3-030-93802-4_8

and interconnection with all living things'. So doing, it transpires, should open up opportunities for a 'transversal alliance today involves non-human agents, technologically-mediated elements, earth-others (land, waters, plants, animals), and non-human inorganic agents (plastic, wires, information highways, algorithms, etc.)' (Braidotti, 2019b, p. 51). Ultimately, what this all makes clear is a strong ethical impetus in posthumanism—one concerned with dismantling any hierarchies otherwise associated with Western modernity. And with regards to the subject matter of this book—deepfakes—the growing inability to distinguish between reality and virtuality as well as the difficulty encountered by human reason in gaining any, let alone privileged, access to the world has become acutely felt and part of the reason why deepfakes have become so disconcerting in public discourse.

Indeed, as Dewandre (2020, p. 4) observes, the modern Cartesian stance not only is focused on (indeed dependent upon) the need for a clear-cut causal explanation of the world but also foregrounds the conviction 'that knowledge is about prediction and control, and that there is no limit to what men can achieve provided they have the will and the knowledge'; in this rendering, freedom equates to autonomy and control, leaving no room for non-human others (and, indeed, for many human others—see e.g. Grear, 2015)—and generative capacities of AI and its underlying technologies, such as deep learning, pose a direct challenge to all of that. The dominant position of this worldview also means that it is typically adopted without questioning by scientists, practitioners, and policymakers alike as the default attitude (Dewandre, 2020, p. 4). However, arguably, instead of transparency and control that one would expect given the dominance of this Cartesian anthropocentrism, the actual condition experienced by the average citizen is increasingly one of surveillance and control—not *by* the subject but *of* the subject (Dewandre, 2020, p. 13). Moreover, as already seen in the discussion on creativity earlier in this book, an increasing gap is opening up between the expectation regarding technology (such as it being concerned with mere tools following strict causal logic and programmers' or a human end-user's commands) and an emergent reality in which artificial agents become increasingly autonomous and original (if not fully creative) actors in their own right (Gervais, 2020, p. 2106). The presence of such increasingly unbridgeable gaps opens one potential pathway for posthumanist thinking to find its way into the public consciousness.

The hubristic nature of anthropocentric thought reveals itself particularly clearly in developmentality studies, whereby human wellbeing is articulated in a peculiar, strongly hierarchical, way: it is assumed that the only kind of human life that can be deemed 'good' is one that is, for the most part, 'freed from the vicissitudes – the risks and vulnerabilities – of living on the planet, of being part of "nature", of being animal'; what development indicators are specifically designed to show, therefore, is the extent of the environmentally embedded and engaged being overcome, rendering the world as an obstacle and not as a co-constitutive part of life (Srinivasan & Kasturirangan, 2016, p. 126). This outlook is also, arguably, a strongly consumption-oriented one. As Srinivasan and Kasturirangan (2016, p. 126) continue, '[e]mbedded in this quest for an insulated and protected life is an ever-increasing degree of consumption – material and otherwise – aimed at enhancing comfort and pleasure, and rendered possible by the use, exploitation and redesign of nonhuman nature' (Srinivasan and Kasturirangan 2016, p. 126). Hence, while humanists 'emphasize the intrinsic and superior value of human beings', thereby exerting violence onto the rest of the world, posthumanists offer a much more fluid worldview, emphasising the blurring of boundaries between what has typically be seen as human and non-human (Coeckelbergh, 2020, pp. 40–42). Broadly, then, post-humanism represents a turn away from human/nature dualisms prevalent in Western philosophy, ultimately aiming to unseat the human as the dominant subject of social enquiry (Margulies & Bersaglio, 2018, p. 103). Digital entities, from simple algorithms to complex AI-powered agents, increasingly contribute to this transformation as well by challenging both seemingly quintessentially human attributes and undermining alleged cognitive capacities that undergird claims to supremacy.

Moreover, it must also be taken into consideration that the anthropocentric perspective of Western modernity naturally leads to demands for preferential care and treatment of humans vis-à-vis the rest of the world: the argument goes that 'as beings who have unique and exceptional qualities, humans deserve a standard of care that exceeds that of other beings', which also means that 'the instrumental use of other beings is acceptable in the pursuit of human wellbeing' (Srinivasan and Kasturirangan 2016, p. 127). In an almost identical way, for Mauthner (2019, p. 679), at the receiving end of posthumanism's critical thrust 'are foundational anthropocentric assumptions underpinning Western philosophy and science whereby the rational and intentional human subject is seen as the locus of epistemological and moral agency, responsibility, and accountability'. Indeed, it should be admitted that the dominant paradigm of the intellectual landscape of Western modernity could, strictly speaking, be summed up 'as a large cultural frame that generates in human beings a feeling of supremacy over the non-human'; this is achieved through a three-tiered fantasy that asserts humans to be ontologically superior as 'special and privileged entities compared to other living beings', epistemologically superior as 'the only sources of knowledge', and ethically superior as 'the sole holders of moral value' (Ferrante & Sartori, 2016, p. 176). The loss of control over reality and the potential for epistemological anarchy ushered in by synthetic media, such as deepfakes, and their potential malevolent (but also to a large extent benevolent) uses definitely contributes to putting such anthropocentric fantasies to question: after all, how could humans justify claims to preferential treatment if the structuration of even the most proximate social environment ends up being a task beyond their capacity.

It is, therefore, the aim of posthumanism to overcome 'the ontological, epistemological, and ethical coordinates of anthropocentrism' by way of critically re-evaluating the relationship between the different—human and non-human—elements of the world in order to weed out the hierarchical anthropocentric perception of reality (Ferrante & Sartori, 2016, p. 177). At the heart of posthumanism, therefore, is 'a refusal to bestow ontological priority, primacy, superiority, or separateness on to *any* ontological being, let alone the human' (Mauthner, 2019, p. 679; see also Barad, 2007). Therefore, posthumanism represents a firmly egalitarian perspective on the crucial issues facing the world today. As such, this perspective is bound to embrace the realisation of the merger of the previously common-sensical reality with an overlay that is no longer 'merely' virtual.

Contrary to popular misperception, posthumanism is not about denial of the human—instead, it is about questioning the taken-for-granted assumptions about the meaning of the 'human' (Herbrechter, 2013, p. 38). According to Braidotti (2013, p. 2), posthumanism, in the same vein, 'introduces a qualitative shift in our thinking about what exactly is the basic unit of common reference for our species, our polity and our relationship to the other inhabitants of this planet', thereby questioning ideas about shared identities—or separate insulated presences, for that matter—when it comes to both everyday practices and the crucial challenges of the day. Lupton and Watson (2020, p. 4), meanwhile, explicitly advocate shifting focus towards 'lively human-data assemblages that are constantly changing as humans move through their everyday worlds, coming to contact with things such as mobile and wearable devices, online software, apps and sensor-embedded environments'. Likewise, for Miller (2020, p. 267), '[p]osthumanism throws open the debate about what makes us human on a number of levels', opening up multiple questions of constitution and causality. In fact, there is nothing natural about the practices of making the world (or, for that matter, the human) as they rely on introducing separations and distinctions that unavoidably raise ethical questions of hierarchy, value, and privilege as well as choices as to how they are best managed (Mauthner, 2019, p. 680). The advent of synthetic media and artificial agents increasingly endowed with creativity certainly raises questions about the possibility of drawing firm lines between human and non-human. At the very least, they render the social domain much more complicated than previously thought by making it more than just inter-human.

To that effect, Roden (2015, p. 124) notes that seen from a posthumanist perspective, actors would be '*functionally autonomous* assemblages', with autonomy referring to the capacity to 'enlist entities as values for functions or accrue functions'. However, such an assertion necessitates vigorous critique—instead of any kind of autonomy, humans should be seen as interrelated within (biological-physical-digital) assemblages that are non-autonomous; in fact, autonomy is most adequately conceived as a humanist vestige as each and every element within them (and entire assemblages as such) are dependent on and co-constituted here and now by myriads of interrelationships; in fact, assuming otherwise would merely be an updated centrism of anthropos-plus (see also Kalpokas, 2021). A much fairer account of the position of the human is provided by Lupton (2020, p. 14) who employs the term 'more than human' to emphasise that 'human bodies/selves are always already distributed phenomena, interembodied with other humans and with nonhumans, multiple and open to the world'. Increasingly, human bodies are also detached from their representations, with virtual versions of the body living their own, often menacing, lives with the help of technology, leaving the physical self and its actions of secondary importance.

Indeed, thinking in terms of assemblages or agglomerations involves threating them not as products but as processes involving many simultaneously interacting components that must themselves be understood as assemblages (DeLanda, 2016, pp. 1–6)—all setting a pattern for understanding the world as a network of interrelated clusters. The reality thereby perceived and understood denotes a world whereby 'assemblages are everywhere, multiplying in every direction, some more viscous and changing at slower speeds, some more fluid and impermanent, coming into being almost as fast as they disappear' (DeLanda, 2016, p. 7). For this reason, it is only natural to focus, as Braidotti and Fuller (2019, p. 7) do, on treating the posthuman (and posthuman-ism) not as a category with clear attributes and a well-worked definition but, instead, as a condition—one that is 'multifarious and finds itself realized in multiple forms across all fields of activity, and all scales of constitution of reality'. In exactly this fashion, the digital environment in which users are increasingly immersing themselves is manifesting an ever-ongoing reconfiguration and rebalancing of the relationship between the human self and its different disembodied versions with limited opportunities to establish authoritativeness and, therefore, hierarchy of presences—all in an ever-ongoing intermingling between humans and technology.

The transformations that make posthumanism particularly acute are, first and foremost, the digital sphere broadly conceived: from the so-called new media to stacks of data and the algorithms crunching them to data centres and the physical infrastructure supporting and connecting them. Taken together, these 'contain an impressive potential for transformations of identity and subjectivity, as well as changes and extensions of experience' that significantly transcend (and simultaneously undermine) 'the traditional individual liberal humanist understanding of the subject' (Herbrechter, 2013, p. 191). However, it is also important not to over-indulge in technological determinism. For example, Mahon (2018, p. 25), in an otherwise rather insightful discussion of posthumanism, provides a characteristic example of this fallacy by asserting that '[p]osthumanism [. . .] takes its basic unit of analysis as humans + tools, where tools would obviously include all forms of technology'. Instead, two crucial clarifications have to be made: first, we have always been posthuman, i.e., embeddedness and interactive becoming has always been the actual condition, with the anthropocentrism of Western modernity being a mere aberration; second, embeddedness within nature must not be ignored either—in fact, it is both chronologically and ontologically a primary form of embeddedness and one can only be ignored in our peril—from the unfolding climate catastrophe to the embeddedness of technology within nature, such as natural resources for hardware production or the massive energy consumption of the entire digital infrastructure (for further elaboration, see Kalpokas, 2021). Hence, even seemingly explicitly virtual phenomena, such as deepfakes (after all, their function is to bring forth something *un*real), must be seen as strongly tied to the ground. Indeed, the latter characteristic of deepfakes—and, more broadly, GANs, CANs, and other underlying technologies—is perilously underexplored. With the ever-growing natural resource requirements (as in e.g. producing hardware necessary for digital agents to operate on) and carbon footprint (production of electricity necessary for training data collection and storage, the generation processes themselves etc.), issues pertaining to the environmental ethics of even benign uses of the technology must be brought to the forefront.

Nevertheless, when it comes to the technological side of embeddedness, one particular segment—AI—could be reasonably seen to stand out. Indeed, whereas traditionally technology was primarily understood as simply an extension of the human, merely *assisting* in both mundane and creative tasks, as tools made for the purpose of expressing human intention rather than their own, AI severely disrupts this understanding, with the potential to undermine it completely (Zatarain, 2017, p. 91). According to Mahon (2018, p. 80), AI is special due to its possession of agency (a claim that, as suggested in the discussion of creativity, is not uncontroversial) but also due to its interactive, learning nature—hence, 'AI listens to us, watches us, responds to us, remembers us, organizes us, answers our queries, communicates for us and to us, makes things for us, entertains us, guides us, transports us – the list could go on and on'. In this sense, it could be suggested that AI 'actively erodes the distinctions between machines, animals and humans', therefore more explicitly than anything else displaying the porous (and, indeed, artificial) nature of distinctions between the different elements that co-constitute the world and their otherwise seemingly taken-for-granted attributes (Mahon, 2018, pp. 80–81). When in comes to synthetic media and artificial creativity, the independent intentiveness of AI, touted by posthumanists, seems to be not yet entirely there—particularly with deepfakes, it is *human* intention—often nefarious—that takes centre stage. Nevertheless, a GAN here is not merely a tool—instead, it is an equal, if not more important, partner, doing what the human would normally be unable to do.

To further hammer down the matter of inseparability and interrelatedness, Lupton (2020, p. 14) places significant emphasis on 'human-data assemblages [that] can be viewed as ever-changing forms of lively materialities' in order to better underscore the embeddedness of humans within their digital surroundings. In this context, it is unsurprising to encounter assertions of 'the blurring of the distinction between reality and virtuality; the blurring of the distinction between human, machine and nature; [. . .] and the shift from the primacy of entities to the primacy of interactions' (The Onlife Initiative, 2015a, p. 7). The self that thus emerges is necessarily embedded, relational, impossible to construe and understand without due reference to the broader enmeshings and interconnections (The Onlife Initiative, 2015a, pp. 11–12). An identical message is also conveyed by Ess (2015, p. 89) who postulates a shift from 'the more *individual* sense of rational-autonomous selfhood characteristic of high modern Western thought' to 'more *relational* senses of selfhood' while Siles et al. (2019, p. 2) stress the importance of 'assemblages of algorithms, platforms, and people' in working out the precise contours of emergence in today's world. Moreover, the patterns of such emergence and the ethical imperatives inherent therein arem multiple—Amoore (2020, p. 165), for example, refers to Spinoza's ethics to help conceptualise the ethical implications of thinking in terms of interrelationships and emergences by stressing the constant ongoingness of 'encounters, arrangements, and combinations' inherent in Spinozist ethical thinking. In today's world, meanwhile, this would translate into a complex pattern of encounters: '[s]ome of these encounters and arrangements involve human beings; others are between unsupervised algorithms and a corpus of data; and more still involve algorithms interacting with other algorithms' (Amoore, 2020, p. 165). One would be hard-pressed to put forward a clearer example of such shared nature of the self than the disentanglement and distribution of the self (and the ability to interact with the multiple disentangled selves of others) offered by synthetic media. The (non-) consensuality of such disentanglements has, of course, become a tricky and potentially dangerous matter.

As it should, hopefully, be evident from the preceding, posthumanist thinking 'contains the aspects of network, complexity and emergence', replacing the metaphysical existence of the self with a more fluid, processual understanding of interaction and (collective) emergence, 'a "becoming human" in connection with an environment and nonhuman actors' (Herbrechter, 2013, p. 206). Meanwhile, Braidotti's (2019a, p. 45) assertion that '[w]e are relational beings, defined by the capacity to affect and be affected' has more than a few overtones of Spinozism and the musings on his notion of *conatus* by authors like Deleuze (1988) and Balibar (1998). In this way, a path is opened up to the recognition that humans are not the only ones possessing agentic capacities but, instead, non-humans (organic and inorganic equally included) have the same; thus, any notion of the non-human 'as passive and inert, requiring external (human) agency to do anything' must be abandoned from both ethical and empirical points of view (Monforte, 2018, p. 380). Unsurprisingly, this shift of focus has the effect of undermining any claim to exclusive human mastery: after all, '[i]f the material world is not simply passive, then our actions will have unpredictable consequences which we may not have wanted and which we may not be able to master'—a point that is crucial and urgent to understand not merely philosophically but also politically, given the dire situation of the natural environment and the growing centrality of the digital space (Choat, 2018, p. 1030). Simultaneously, this unpredictability of consequences acquires an additional facet in relation to deepfakes: in terms of the digital doppelgangers of individuals that today stalk the digital space by default, the possibility is opened up for their mutation into new cyborg entities—in part, mere digitised reflections of the self but simultaneously also technologized remakings of the self; in terms of data, though, while the unpredictability of used of personal data has been a major point of concern for quite a while already, the possibility of openly nefarious versions of the self being created takes such problematic to a whole new level.

In a fashion rather similar to the above, Barad (2003, p. 818) has also attempted to reconfigure agency, defining it as 'not an attribute but the ongoing reconfigurings of the world'. At the same time, though, such permanent becoming must also be seen as not exclusive to humans. Instead, as insightfully noted by Mauthner (2019, p. 671), 'the world is not composed of preexisting and already-formed entities awaiting discovery by human knowers'; rather, the same process of dynamic and interactive emergence takes place around contexts, and any attempt to uncover an 'essence' only ends up in an artificial fixation of a fleeting moment within a constant flux—in a way, this means that the world which is studied is brought into existence by the very act of studying it (see also Barad, 2007). This unavoidably leads to embracing the fact that all cognition is, in the end, situated and impossible to either gain or understand outside its proper context (Heras-Escribano, 2019, p. 19). In a non-dissimilar fashion, for Greene (2013, p. 753), research conducted in a posthumanist fashion can be described as '*dynamic, fluid, indefinite, unfolding*', rejecting fixed and bounded characteristics of the subject and process but, instead, 'fleeting and fluid, propelled by lines of flight'. Braidotti (2019a, p. 47) concurs with such a position my stressing that 'posthuman subjects of knowledge and embedded, embodied and yet flowing in a web of relations with human and non-human others'. In fact, one could go as far as to assert that 'the world is ontologically indeterminate outside specific practices and entails knowledge practices accounting for themselves and their world-making effects', meaning that the main point of concern is not even humans as such but the capacity they have for bringing into existence different determinate configurations of the world (Mauthner, 2019, pp. 680–681). This indeterminacy of the world also helps better understand the disturbing nature of epistemological anarchy to which deepfakes contribute. While the commonplace assertions of Western modernity imply the need for clear-cut knowledge of the world that is seen as objectively and tangibly existing, the recognition of a murky and unpredictable reality made pressing by synthetic media becomes a posthumanist act par excellence. By implication, then, such anarchic condition is only going to deepen as the human-technology-nature indistinction extends further (which is yet another reason not to see deepfakes as a mere aberration).

As is clear form the above, one must unavoidably start questioning qualities like the decision-making capacity of humans as well as their capacity for unaffected judgement and self-determination. Lupton (2020, p. 18), for example, enlists a broad range of interdependencies by calling for 'a more-than-human consideration of the ways in which the enfleshed affordances of human bodies – their sensory percep-tions, thoughts, memories, desires, imaginings, physical movements and feelings – come together with digital technologies' and do so in multiple ways and capacities that may or may not lead to the expected results and uses. Very similarly, for Braidotti (2013, p. 62), the human self has been strongly put into question by 'life-mining' and 'visibility, predictability and exportability' while Sandvik (2020, p. 4) calls for taking into greater consideration the nonhuman summands of human-technology interactions that include, among other things, 'device parameters and affordances, analytical algorithms, data infrastructure, and data itself, as well as the processes and practices around [devices]'. Meanwhile, Ammerman (2019, p. 172) touches upon a rather similar field of concerns in a rather blunter fashion by simply asserting that '[w]e must start asking ourselves if our behaviors are the product of nature, nurture, or neural networks'. Should one adopt this perspective, it becomes unsurprising that references to 'cyborg' have become increasingly prevalent in describing the human-technology relationship, particularly ways in which both human body and action are becoming inseparable from technological apparatuses of the most varied definition (Miller, 2020, p. 269). As a way of drawing attention to the growing human-machine interdependence, 'the notion of the cyborg can be seen as a kind of relationship describing the interface between humans and technology', ultimately leading to a convergence of both into a composite entity 'that has unique properties not available to either' (Miller, 2020, p. 269). Moreover, one could also stress the increasing 'decorporealisation' of the individual as another form of cyborgisation, whereby the individual is distributed across multiple data doubles that stand in for that person in various contexts, adding as digital datafied extensions of the self that are never identical to the self either (Hepp, 2020, p. 159). Likewise, as mentioned above, one's data and digital reflections (in the form of images, videos etc.) stored across the vastness of the digital space become cyborg entities as well—entanglements of elements reminiscent of the original self and technological extensions, re-renderings, and overlays. In this way, should affective capacity (drawing from the Spinozist musings of Amoore and Braidotti above) be concerned, the ability to affect and be affected becomes increasingly difficult to separate from the cyborgisation effects of GANs and other digital technologies.

Simultaneously, though, one should not focus on the digital environment as some form of external determining force—after all, that would be against the posthumanist focus on horizontal interconnections and, therefore, simply replace anthropocentrism with technocentrism (see, generally, Kalpokas, 2021). A similar point is also made by Pentzhold and Bischof (2019, p. 7) who have criticised essentialist ascriptions of agency to either humans or technology for failing to take into account 'the association of people and robots in the collective accomplishment of affordances', particularly in cases where shared and collectively situated actions are at stake'. Indeed, such affordances, understood first and foremost as 'the possibilities for action' only have meaning and for and become negotiated by particular actors in their particular environments (Heras-Escribano, 2019, p. 3). Instead, an interactive two-way relationship should be emphasised here as well as it is not just digital artefacts affecting and structuring the human but also humans affecting and structuring the digital by way of data feedback loops that feed back into computational processes. After all, as Amoore (2019, p. 152) observes, 'computations are infinitely malleable and contingent on plural interactions of humans and algorithms', meaning that even 'a small change in the weighting of probabilities in the model will transform the output signal and, therefore, the decision'. The implication is also that the ultimate and exhausting resolution of competing accounts of reality and a settlement on an ultimate view of the world is impossible; hence, 'there is no unified authorial source of truth, but rather a distributed and oblique account of the impossibility of resolving truthfulness before the public' (Amoore, 2019, p. 158). If that is the case, then doubt becomes the default epistemological condition. As Amoore (2019, p. 163) continues, posthuman subjects are unavoidably doubtful and 'dwell uneasily within partial and situated knowledges and, when they make a claim in the world, they do so in ways that stray from calculable paths'. Such doubtfulness should then be best seen as the consequence of interconnectedness between humans and their counterparts as it 'expresses the many ways in which algorithms dwell within us, just as we too dwell as data and test subjects within their layers' (Amoore, 2019, p. 163). The main challenge facing us in this kind of interactive relationship is making it equitable and as robust and immune to abuse as possible. Thus far, existing regulatory frameworks provide only a partial answer to this question and further attempts, and finding the right balance between innovation and the necessity to ensure a symbiotic, rather than parasitic, model of human-digital interaction should be made a priority.

In a non-unrelated way, Braidotti (2019b, p. 48) puts forward 'complexity' as the keyword; for her, one should turn attention to a conception of the subject as 'a complex singularity, an affective assemblage, and a relational vitalist entity'. Hence, affordances and interactive capacities of the elements within agglomerations can never be predetermined or even foreseen but, instead, 'are collectively achieved in interactions between human and technological agents'; moreover, being best understood as achievements, such affordances are never simply discovered (hence, they are not a matter of hindsight either) but, instead, emerge in the here and now, in the interplay between the different summands of human-natural-technological agglomerations (Pentzhold & Bischof, 2019, pp. 5–6). In this way, transcending the distinction between humans and machines becomes a matter not of hubristic accounts of scientific progress or transhumanist fantasies of machine-enabled omnipotence and immortality but, rather, part of an ethical egalitarian impetus (Coeckelbergh, 2020, pp. 42–43). Likewise, this opens up the possibility to conceive of future developments in a non-anthropocentric fashion, such as giving the opportunity for AI to 'free itself of the burden to imitate or rebuild the human' and, instead, 'explore different, non-human kinds of being, intelligence, creativity, and so on' (Coeckelbergh, 2020, p. 43). Within the ambit of this book, 'liberation' of AI most immediately pertains to the domain of AI creativity and questions of agency embedded therein. Indeed, instead of focusing on AI-produced content as unsettling and uncanny or detached from (or, at best, merely parasitic on) the human cultural context, one should see AI as *the* cultural context of today and as the only agent actually capable of giving expressions to the datafied human-digital enmeshings that characterise today's world.

Complexity also extends into the core of interrelatedness between humans and the digital environment. Here, Amoore (2020, p. 8) makes an important observation that '[a]lgorithms come to act in the world precisely in and through the relations of selves to selves, and selves to others, as these relations are manifest in the clusters and attributes of data'. In other words, the relationships and identities that come to act in this world arise within the triangle of humans, algorithms, and data, ultimately underpinning any shared sense of the world. However, this is also a relationship that is constantly interactively morphing through the effects that such data-based relating has on humans, the data in question being updated to reflect those effects through constant processes of datafication, and the algorithms themselves changing courtesy to machine learning techniques. Indeed, any knowledge produced, affordances negotiated, or agency enabled can only be explained as an emergent condition 'situated in the lively web of interdependencies' (Cielemęcka & Daigle, 2019, p. 81). Perhaps the most characteristic expression of such lively interdependencies can be found in AI's attempts at human portraiture. While it is relatively easy to treat the almost 'faceless' portraits generated by CAN—distorted by the variety of portraits in the training data—as lacking an understanding of the human and of the intricate cultural context that goes into a portrait (see e.g. Bogost, 2019), the matter should be seen in exactly the opposite way—such shaped and twisted portraits are *precisely* the perfect allegory for today's world of ever-ongoing human-digital interactions in which the data-based reflections of the self are never mirror-like or even photographic but, instead, ever-changing, distorted (due to incompleteness of or imprecisions in data) but also *distortable* (as in creation of synthetic media such as deepfakes). Overall, then, interactive indeterminacy of the self must be the backdrop against which deepfakes and their underlying technologies must be evaluated.

References

Ammerman, W. (2019). *The invisible brand: Marketing in the age of automation, big data, and machine learning*. McGraw-Hill.

Amoore, L. (2019). Doubt and the algorithm: On the partial accounts of machine learning. *Theory, Culture & Society, 36*(6), 147–169.

Amoore, L. (2020). *Cloud ethics: Algorithms and the attributes of ourselves and others*. Duke University Press.

Balibar, E. (1998). *Spinoza and politics*. Verso.

Barad, K. (2003). Posthumanist performativity: Toward an understanding of how matter comes to matter. *Signs, 28*(3), 801–831.

Barad, K. (2007). *Meeting the universe halfway: Quantum physics and the entanglement of matter and meaning*. Duke University Press.

Bogost, I. (2019, March 6). The AI-art gold rush is here. *The Atlantic*, https://www.theatlantic.com/technology/archive/2019/03/ai-created-art-invades-chelsea-gallery-scene/584134/

Braidotti, R. (2013). *The Posthuman*. Polity Press.

Braidotti, R. (2019a). *Posthuman knowledge*. Polity.

Braidotti, R. (2019b). A theoretical framework for the critical posthumanities. *Theory, Culture & Society, 36*(6), 31–61.

Braidotti, R., & Fuller, M. (2019). The posthumanities in an era of unexpected consequences. *Theory, Culture & Society, 36*(6), 3–29.

Chandler, D. (2015). A world without causation: Big data and the coming of age of posthumanism. *Millennium: Journal of International Studies, 43*(3), 833–851.

Choat, S. (2018). Science, agency and ontology: A historical-materialist response to new materialism. *Political Studies, 66*(4), 1027–1042.

Cielemęcka, O., & Daigle, C. (2019). Posthuman sustainability: An ethos for our anthropocenic future. *Theory, Culture & Society, 36*(7–8), 67–87.

Coeckelbergh, M. (2020). *AI ethics*. The MIT Press.

DeLanda, M. (2016). *Assemblage theory*. Edinburgh University Press.

Deleuze, G. (1988). *Spinoza: Practical philosophy*. City Lights Books.

Dewandre, N. (2020). Big data: From modern fears to enlightened and vigilant embrace of new beginnings. *Big Data & Society*. https://doi.org/10.1177/2053951720936708

Ess, C. (2015). The onlife manifesto: Philosophical backgrounds, media usages, and the futures of democracy and equality. In L. Floridi (Ed.), *The onlife manifesto: Being human in a hyperconnected era* (pp. 89–109). Springer.

Ferrante, A., & Sartori, D. (2016). From anthropocentrism to post-humanism in the educational debate. *Relations, 4*(2), 175–194.

Gervais, D. J. (2020). The machine as author. *Iowa Law Review, 105*, 2053–2106.

Grear, A. (2015). Deconstructing *Anthropos*: a critical legal reflection on 'Anthropocentric' law and anthropocene 'Humanity'. *Law Critique, 26*, 225–249.

Greene, J. C. (2013). On rhizomes, lines of flight, mangles, and other assemblages. *International Journal of Qualitative Studies in Education, 26*(6), 749–458.

Hepp, A. (2020). *Deep mediatization*. Routledge.

Heras-Escribano, M. (2019). *The philosophy of affordances*. Palgrave Macmillan.

Herbrechter, S. (2013). *Posthumanism: A critical analysis*. Bloomsbury.

Kalpokas, I. (2021). *Malleable, digital, and posthuman: A permanently beta life*. Emerald.

Lupton, D. (2020). *Data selves*. Polity.

Lupton, D., & Watson, A. (2020). Towards more-than-human digital data studies: Developing research-creation methods. *Qualitative Research*. https://doi.org/10.1177/1468794120939235

Mahon, P. (2018). *Posthumanism: A guide for the perplexed*. Bloomsbury.

Margulies, J. D., & Bersaglio, B. (2018). Furthering post-human political ecologies. *Geoforum, 94*, 103–106.

Mauthner, N. S. (2019). Toward a posthumanist ethics of qualitative research in a big data era. *American Behavioral Scientist, 63*(6), 669–698.

Miller, V. (2020). *Understanding digital culture* (2nd ed.). SAGE Publications.

Monforte, J. (2018). What is new for New Materialism for a Newcomer. *Qualitative Research in Sport, Exercise and Health, 10*(3), 378–390.

Pentzhold, C., & Bischof, A. (2019). Making affordances real: Socio-material prefiguration, performed agency, and coordinated activities in human-robot communication. *Social Media + Society*. https://doi.org/10.1177/2056305119865472

Roden, D. (2015). *Posthuman life: Philosophy at the edge of the human*. Routledge.

Sandvik, K. B. (2020). Wearables for something good: Aid, dataveillance and the production of children's digital bodies. *Information, Communication & Society*. https://doi.org/10.1080/1369118X.2020.1753797

Siles, I., Espinoza-Rojas, J., Naranjo, A., & Tristán, M. F. (2019). The mutual domestication of users and algorithmic recommendation on netflix. *Communication, Culture & Critique*. https://doi.org/10.1093/ccc/tcz025

Srinivasan, K., & Kasturirangan, R. (2016). Political ecology, development and human exceptionalism. *Geoforum, 75*, 125–128.

The Onlife Initiative. (2015a). The onlife manifesto. In L. Floridi (Ed.), *The onlife manifesto: being human in a hyperconnected era* (pp. 7–13). Springer.

The Onlife Initiative. (2015b). Background document: Rethinking public spaces in the digital transition. In L. Floridi (Ed.), *The onlife manifesto: Being human in a hyperconnected era* (pp. 41–47). Springer.

Zatarain, J. M. N. (2017). The role of automated technology in the creation of copyright works: The challenges of artificial intelligence. *International Review of Law, Computers & Technology, 31*(1), 91–104.

Chapter 9
Conclusion

The aim of this book has been to provide a nuanced and realistic assessment of deepfakes by exploring their most proximate environment, including technological underpinnings and the broad transformations of the media environment while also extending the thought process towards broader, more general developments, such as those encapsulated by posthumanist thought. In doing so, a picture emerges of deepfakes that can be, and in many ways are, dangerous, possessing the potential if not to undermine entire political systems, then at least to destroy individual lives, but also manifesting potentially beneficial uses and even representing important societal and cultural shifts, e.g. towards algorithmic creativity. They are also illustrative of broader transformations of our societies—most notably, involving a thrust towards deprivileging the human self. As such, deepfakes are perhaps less dramatic (in the headline-grabbing sense) but, in fact, significantly more interesting and intriguing than previously conceived.

Deepfakes are at their most fundamental in very explicitly decoupling the relationship between the human self and its many digital doppelgangers or data doubles. Of course, even prior to deepfakes, there was great importance in discussing the adequacy of such data doubles and their interactive nature of forming, and not just merely representing, individuals. It was, and still is, the case that the data doubles, or digital representations of users cobbled together by social media, search, and other platforms 'feed back into real lives and entail palpable material consequences' affecting the users the digital effigies of whom they are supposed to be and thereby becoming 'constitutive of what they allegedly merely represent' (Pötzsch, 2018, p. 3317). It is likewise still correct that content selection and targeting of content has in itself become 'a growing source of and factor in social order' and in the construction of social realities (Just & Latzer, 2017, p. 254). What is different this time is that the digital doubles are very visibly (in the closest sense that one could approximate a digital embodiment) and very openly unmoored from the pretence of representing an underlying human self and, with the help of synthetic media, begin living their own, potentially uncontrollable and unpredictable, cyborg lives.

© The Author(s), under exclusive license to Springer Nature Switzerland AG 2022   85
I. Kalpokas, J. Kalpokiene, *Deepfakes*, SpringerBriefs in Political Science,
https://doi.org/10.1007/978-3-030-93802-4_9

Another way in which the account of deepfakes presented in this book builds upon and furthers existing research is in terms of focus on the productive capacities of digital tools and artefacts. In the usual sense, one would discuss the 'productive capacities' of algorithms exceeding mere mediation of the world in terms of making users largely dependent on the code that constructs and sustains platform architecture, ultimately seeing algorithms as 'making a difference in how social formations and relations are formed' (Bucher, 2018, pp. 72–73). In this way, the human-algorithm relationship would have been primarily focused on a dual nature of today's life as having 'a frontend (the world we see and navigate) and a backend (the largely invisible computational architecture that sustains and informs the frontend)' (Hildebrandt, 2016, p. 5), thereby dismantling the supposed normality and self-evidence of digitally structured life (see e.g. Greenfield, 2018, p. 212). What the focus on deepfakes and their potential to contribute to epistemic anarchy reveals is precisely the opposite to algorithmic productivity-qua-structuration. Instead, this book demonstrates the potential of digital tools and artefacts to bring the seemingly orderly world apart and introduce indeterminacy and doubt into the digital environment that had still, on surface at least, been compliant with the dominant attitudes of Western modernity (for more on doubt as an epistemological foundation, see e.g. Philippopuoulos-Mihalopoulos, 2015).

On the other hand, as stressed in the final chapter of this book, the anarchic and doubt-laden nature of the digital environment (and, by implication, increasingly of the physical environment as well) is not something newly emergent but, instead, a permanent underlying feature that is only now being laid bare. Even outside posthumanist perspectives, some authors would go as far as to completely deny human ability to adequately perceive and understand the real world—for them, the world we encounter is merely an interface developed through evolution for interacting in the environment in ways that maximise chances of survival, at the expense of truth if necessary (see, notably, Hoffman, 2019). Under this view, we perceive and understand the world in the peculiarly human way 'not because we reconstruct objective reality, but because this is the format of a compression algorithm that evolution happened to build into us' and we clearly know that other species have different 'data formats' to compress and understand information about the world; hence, we effectively misrecognise a data compression format with objective reality (Hoffman, 2019, pp. 117–118). To paraphrase some useful analogies given by Hoffman (2019), we navigate the world as we do computer desktop—by interacting with icons that are by no means the real thing but, instead, interfaces for the computational procedures and hardware performances necessary to carry out the desired action; similarly, when playing a computer game, we may feel transported into the game world, but the computer graphics we interact with do not constitute a real world—instead, it is the unseen code, hardware, and the electrical currents that that constitute the 'objective' game world. Should we accept this idea, anthropocentric world-mastery would be even physiologically and neurologically impossible.

Such an assertion might appear to be rather far-fetched should we imagine the human self as premised upon a rich inner world and having unique mastery over the lived environment. However, as it has already been shown, such a view would be erroneous – instead, both human and machine intelligence transpires to be based on learning processes that take place on the go. In fact, Charter (2019, p. 5) goes even further to underscore the point: crucially, 'introspection is a process not of *perception* but of *invention*, whereby '[t]he inner world is a mirage', leading to the assertion that, speaking of the human mind, '[t]he truth is not that the depths are empty, or even shallow, but that the surface is all there is'. In this sense, it is quite likely that we are living through a period that is characterised not by an unfolding infocalypse but simply by an update in the interface through which we perceive and interact with what is typically conceived of as 'reality'.

To sum up, the digital transformations, exemplified, among other things, by synthetic media of which deepfakes are a significant part open up and lay bare the necessity to engage with 'the diversity of inextricably bound relationships that exist along ontological, spatial, and temporal lines' and 'the unpredictable, non-linear nature of events' (Gellers, 2021, p. 2). In so doing, they certainly contribute to better understanding the emergent features of the increasingly virtual-first life to come.

References

Bucher, T. (2018). *If... Then: Algorithmic power and politics*. Oxford University Press.

Charter, N. (2019). *The mind is flat: The illusion of mental depth and the improvised mind*. Yale University Press.

Gellers, J. C. (2021). Earth system law and the legal status of non-humans in the anthropocene. *Earth System Governance*. https://doi.org/10.1016/j.esg.2020.100083

Greenfield, A. (2018). *Radical technologies: The design of everyday life*. Verso.

Hildebrandt, M. (2016). Law *as* information in the era of data-driven agency. *The Modern Law Review, 79*(1), 1–30.

Hoffman, D. D. (2019). *The case against reality: How evolution hid the truth from our eyes*. Allen Lane.

Just, N., & Latzer, M. (2017). Governance by algorithms: Reality construction by algorithmic selection in the internet. *Media, Culture & Society, 39*(2), 238–258.

Philippopuoulos-Mihalopoulos, A. (2015). Epistemologies of doubt. In A. Grear & L. J. Kotzé (Eds.), *Research handbook on Human Rights and the environment* (pp. 28–45). Edward Elgar.

Pötzsch, H. (2018). Archives and identity in the context of social media and algorithmic analytics: Towards an understanding of iarchive and predictive retention. *New Media & Society, 20*(9), 3304–3322.

Printed in the United States
by Baker & Taylor Publisher Services